PRAISE FOR C

Anselm Stolz (1900–1942), ha-
lia, was Professor of Systematic Theology at ᴗaᴜᴄᴛᴀᴍᴏᴇ.. ne
from 1928 until his early death. His thesis on the Creed in St Thomas
Aquinas, which also took Rousselot's work into consideration, the
six volumes of his *Handbook of Dogmatics* based on the experience of
Divine Wisdom, and his famous *Theologie Der Mystik* (1936) marked
him out as belonging to those post First World War authors who
were expecting a revival of spiritual and fundamental theology, i.e.
the reconnection of *fides qua* and *fides quae*, the faith as received
and lived and the faith which the Church believes. The separation of
these two, present since the Modernist crisis, would thus be overcome.
Stolz argued for a transformation of man, in his ontological depths, on
his sacramental and ascetic journey. Mager and many French authors
argued in addition for a psychologically verifiable change in the inner
man, another type of experience of self and God in the depths and
heights of human understanding. *Ascesi christiana* is the final stage
of Stolz's journey towards the perfection which lies deep within man,
which is at the same time beyond his capabilities. The most important
authors in the field of this controversy were Augustin Poulain, A. San-
dreau, Pierre Pourrat, Joseph de Guibert, Laurent Reypens, Maurice
de la Taille, Ambroise Gardeil, Reginald Garrigou-Lagrange, and also
the early Karl Rahner, Hans Urs von Balthasar and Henri de Lubac.
It was the beginning of spiritual and fundamental theology as new
disciplines in academic theology. It was no coincidence that the DSP
(*Dictionary of Spirituality*) was also launched at this time. It took 65
years for the last volume of this work to appear, time during which
the character of the work no doubt changed.
  —**FR. ELMAR SALMANN**, OSB, Professor of Philosophy and
Systematic Theology at the Pontifical University St. Anselm (Rome),
Pontifical Gregorian University (Rome) and at the Hochschule für
Philosophie (München)

The Benedictine scholar Anselm Stolz is well known for establishing
the biblical, patristic, sacramental, and monastic roots of Christian
mysticism. The present book, spiritual conferences Fr Stolz deliv-
ered at the threshold of the Second World War, completes his task.
Here we learn that the ascetical life, forged and tested by hermits, is
the touchstone of Christian perfection. As witnesses in the heart of
the Church, hermits point the way to service and love of the King
whose kingdom, though not of this world, renews this world wherever
asceticism is truly tried. Fr Giles Conacher, OSB, has performed a
great service in retrieving this work and rendering it in English with

fidelity and grace. *Christian Asceticism* is an essential document in the history of ascetic and mystical theology and a landmark in the twentieth-century renewal of Catholic and monastic thought.
— **CAROL ZALESKI**, Professor of World Religions, Smith College, Northampton, Mass., author of *Otherworld Journeys: Accounts of Near-Death Experience in Medieval and Modern Times* (Oxford University Press) and other titles.

Christian Asceticism

Christian Asceticism

ANSELM STOLZ, OSB
*Professor of Systematic Theology at
Sant'Anselmo in Rome (1928–1942)*

Translated by
GILES CONACHER, OSB
Monk of Pluscarden Abbey

Introduction by
DONATO OGLIARI, OSB
✠ *Archabbot and Ordinary of Montecassino*

Foreword by
ROBERTO FERRARI, OSB
*Researcher in Mystical and
Monastic Spiritual Theology*

AROUCA PRESS

Based on a series of lectures given at Chevetogne in 1939
Originally published in French in 1948
by Editions des Bénédictins d'Amay

Copyright © Monastère de Chevetogne 2021
Translation © Giles Conacher, OSB 2021
Introduction © Donato Ogliari, OSB
Foreword © Roberto Ferrari, OSB

All rights reserved:
No part of this book may be reproduced or transmitted,
in any form or by any means, without permission

ISBN: 978-1-989905-70-8 (pbk)
ISBN: 978-1-989905-71-5 (hardcover)

Arouca Press
PO Box 55003
Bridgeport PO
Waterloo, ON N2J 3G0
Canada
www.aroucapress.com

Send inquiries to info@aroucapress.com

CONTENTS

Abbreviations ix
Translator's Dedication and Acknowledgements. . . . xi
Preface to the Italian edition xiii
Preface to the French Edition. xv
Introduction. xxiii
Foreword. xxv

1 The Hermit Life 1
2 Other Forms of the Ascetic Life 23
3 Imitation of Christ. 39
4 The Ascetic as Martyr 61
5 The Soldier of Jesus Christ 75
6 Silence 87
7 The Life of Prayer 93
8 Liturgy and Personal Devotion. 109
9 Holy Scripture. 127
10 The Ascetic as Apostle. 141

Epilogue 155
About the Translator. 159

ABBREVIATIONS

Dial. *St. Gregory the Great: Dialogues.* Translated by Odo John Zimmerman OSB, FOTC vol. 39, CUA Press in association with Consortium Books, Washington DC, 1959

RB *RB1980 - The Rule of St. Benedict*, ed. Timothy Fry OSB, Liturgical Press, Collegeville, MN, 1980

PG *Patrologia Graeca*, ed. J. P. Migne, 1–161, Paris, 1857–1886

FOTC *Fathers of the Church* series, Catholic University of America Press, Washington DC

TRANSLATOR'S DEDICATION AND ACKNOWLEDGEMENTS

I WOULD LIKE TO DEDICATE THIS TRANSlation to my brethren, who have borne with me and encouraged me, and more especially to Prior Bede Kierney and the monks of Kristo Buase Monastery, Techiman, Ghana, under whose hospitable roof the initial translation was made. Then thanks to D. Roberto Ferrari OSB, for the Foreword and Archabbot Donato Ogliari OSB for the Introduction. Br Isidore Colm OSB, Sr Maria Edith Renfrew, Erem. Dio., Bishop Hugh Gilbert OSB, Fr. Edmund Power OSB, Fr Dunstan Robertson OSB, Fr. Elmar Salmann OSB, Irene and Claude Wischik, Carol and Philip Zaleski and many Francophone brothers and sisters have helped me and contributed in various ways; Eileen Grant took on the task of editing and finally, Alex Barbas accepted the book.

Giles Conacher OSB

PREFACE TO THE ITALIAN EDITION

THE AUTHOR OF THESE PAGES WAS ONE of those indefatigable workers of the spirit whom the Lord calls to himself in the full vigour of his forces and activity. Dom Anselm Stolz had scarcely reached 43 years of age, 22 years of monastic life, 18 of priesthood, 14 of theological teaching, which to human eyes seems far too short a space of time for a man so richly endowed. The Lord, however, and He alone, decides when a man has fulfilled his span.

Dom Anselm Stolz was born on 28th January 1900 at Erkrath near Dusseldorf in Germany. Having finished high school at Dusseldorf, he consecrated himself to Benedictine life at the Abbey of Gerleve in Westphalia on 29th February 1920. He was sent to study at Rome, where he obtained a doctorate in theology. There the young monk spent 20 years, first as a student, then as a professor at the Pontifical Academic Institute of Sant'Anselmo, years very fertile in study and priestly activity, until the morning of 19th October 1942, when he peacefully surrendered his soul into the hands of the heavenly Father.

The pages which follow are the last work, the final teaching and admonitions of a venerated Master. *Christian Asceticism* which is here presented is the diligently worked out fruit of meditations, researches and discussions on the ideal of Christian perfection; this reveals one of the central characteristics of Stolz's theology.

Therefore, may the pages which we now put before you produce the fruit desired by the author; may they be a real consolation and help to souls on the arduous path of return to the heavenly Father. And may the departed receive the just reward of eternal life, given to those who after serving the Lord with complete dedication, loosed from the bonds of the flesh, may contemplate God, no longer in shadows and appearances, but face to face, as He is.

The publishers

PREFACE TO THE FRENCH EDITION

IT IS NOT OUR INTENTION HERE TO SET forth a complete ascetical theology. Had this been our goal, it would have been necessary to deal with many other questions, and there is no lack of solid works on the subject in current literature. Our aim was to set forth some essential concepts relative to the ascetical life, according to the tradition of the ancient Fathers. Nor is this the place to look for teaching of directly practical intent. Rather, our aim has been to bring out certain aspects of the ascetical life which, though very important, are sometimes somewhat forgotten. It is up to the spiritual director to apply to individuals the principles which we are about to set forth.

It might be that what we are going to say about the ascetical life could lead to discouragement: is not the ideal we are setting out too high, quite inaccessible to poor human nature? And yet, those who put these principles into practice were flesh and blood, just like us, and experienced our weaknesses. Admittedly we cannot imitate the ancient Fathers in everything; today, some of their ideas and practices seem exaggerated to us. It will nonetheless be very useful to give some thought to these, since they will help us understand what, in the Church's tradition, must be considered as essential to the mystical life.

No-one nowadays could think of leading a hermit life like some of the fourth century Fathers; for example, no one would decide to imitate the life of St Simeon, "mad for Christ", in every detail. And yet, have the saints of the following centuries always limited themselves to what human reason can grasp and make sense of? Their lives are not, for all that, any less exemplary for us. The same is true of the saints of antiquity. They shone a light on the great principles of Christian life and asceticism, even if, at times, their application of them was too rigid. The Desert Fathers themselves were, after all, conscious of the considerable changes which the outward form of the ascetical life would have to undergo. In the *Apophthegms*, the *Sayings*, monastic writings of the early ages, the following story is told:

The holy Fathers were prophesying about the last times. One day they asked, "What have we ourselves done?" One of them, the great Abba Ischyrion, replied, "We have kept the commandments of God." "And what will the ones who come after us do?" asked the others. Ischyrion replied, "They will not manage to do half of what we have done." The Fathers went on, 'And what of those who will come after them?" The Abba replied, "The men of that era will not be very rich in good works; the time of the great trial will arise against them, and those who in that age will be found good, will be greater than we and our Fathers."[1]

You will seek in vain, in this modest work of ours, for a chapter dealing with some of the great Christian virtues, in particular humility, obedience, etc. We have, nonetheless, tried to show the theological foundation of these virtues and their roots in the ascetical ideal.

Some may think that this ideal too single-mindedly emphasizes monastic asceticism, and that in that way it excludes most Christians living in the world. That does not tie in with the facts. The ascetical ideal is the same for all; only circumstances and the means for its attainment differ. If we have here limited ourselves to describing the ascetical life in its most extreme and logical forms, and to some extent in its historical development, that is so as to bring out its essence more clearly.

After all, everyone knows that detachment from the world, renouncing self-will, humility and the other virtues are part of asceticism, but very rarely are people aware of what constitutes its very essence. It is of primary importance, both for the monk-ascetic and for one who lives in the world, to see clearly what that is. The essence is central in every case, even if the ascetical life is being led amid the world.

It is not easy to sum up the essence of the ascetical life in one word. One could rightly say that it consists in the imitation of Christ. If it is to be correctly understood, this reply, though entirely true, presupposes a theological culture going beyond the

1 *Apophthegmata Patrum* PG 65, 241D; Vitae Patrum I, 14–(59) De abbate Ischyrione

Preface to the French Edition

average. Another reply, arising from the previous one, could be that being an ascetic means being a soldier of Christ, renouncing your will in order to follow Christ as your King, to do battle under his standard, using the weapons of obedience. In the prologue to his Rule, St Benedict presents the ascetical ideal in this way. He talks of renunciation, military service, weapons. Why? All these ideas must have a common root and rationale.

Our problem could to some extent be compared to the question the Philippians asked St Paul about the essence of the Christian life. St Paul, forced to clarify his thought, replied,

> Whatever is true, whatever is honourable, whatever is just, whatever is pure, whatever is pleasing, whatever is commendable, if there is any excellence and if there is anything worthy of praise, think about those things. Keep on doing the things that you have learned and received and heard and seen in me, and the God of peace will be with you (Phil. 4:8–9).

This text shows us clearly that people at Philippi were debating the value of pagan virtue and the good that those did who were outside the Church. What was to be the Christians' attitude to this? Were they to give their approval to all these foreign theories and practices? The Apostle replied, Beware of noisy words, weigh them carefully first of all. But above all, do what you have seen me doing. So the saint insists on the value of apostolic example, more important for the Christian life than speculation and subtle discussions.

We could apply the same principle to our own problem. It will be more useful for us to refer to the example of Christian ascetics than any discussion, if we seek to arrive at a clear notion of the essence of the ascetical life; in that way the ideal which dominated their ascesis throughout their whole lives will become clear to us. It would be enough, for example, to study the life of St Benedict, the great patriarch of Western monks. It was written by St Gregory the Great, himself an ascetic and monk, in order to demonstrate just how the ascetical and monastic life was the same in the West as it was in the East. Besides the fact that it represents a notable part of the ascetical tradition, that life takes on particular importance from the fact that is not just a simple "history", but simultaneously an illustration and interpretation of an ideal. This is why we will have occasion to make frequent reference to it in the pages which follow.

Limiting ourselves to this life alone, would however, be setting our horizon too narrowly, given our goal. For this account itself requires, from many points of view, interpretation drawn from other sources of ascetical teaching, namely the biographies and teachings of the ancient anchorites and monks, and the body of theological teaching of the Church of bygone ages. This becomes clear as soon as we face up to the first question raised by St Benedict's life, that is to say, the young ascetic's decision to withdraw into the desert.

St Benedict was already leading a life apart, made up of prayer and mortification, but this as a member of the Church at Enfide. He was even part of its staff. But when his first miracle revealed his great virtue, he resolved to give up this service and went and lived apart in a desert place. His biographer tells us, "St Benedict sought suffering more than praise; he preferred to wear himself out in the works of God than to be filled with life's favours."[2] And indeed, this was the immediate motive which impelled him to embrace the hermit life. This is not, however, the motive which underlies every anchorite vocation. That needs deeper and more universal foundations. And since Christian antiquity saw the hermit life as one of the most important forms of ascetical life, we will need to look for those deeper reasons which led those first ascetics to adopt it. We think that here we are dealing with something that is essential for a better understanding of the ascetic teaching of the ancients. The hermit way of life was not something passing, but rather the clearest expression of every ascetic quest during the classical era of Christian asceticism. So it is that our investigation of the eremitical life underlies the whole of this study, since we will more easily be able to rediscover, in this form of life which was so important and so universally esteemed in the ancient Church, the concept which was the basis of all Christian asceticism. In our view, that fundamental

---

[2] *Dial.* II, 1, p. 57

concept was summed up in the idea of complete separation from the world, in order to be able to give oneself to God with greater freedom. The Christian ascetic is essentially someone who frees himself from the world; he is *extra mundum factus*, he moves outside the world.

In beginning this account of the hermit life, we are not advocating that every ascetic should embrace such a way of life. Nor do we even maintain that this form of life ought always to be in the Church, nor that it suits every age and every place. We want simply to say that the hermit life is the logical outcome of the ascetical teaching of the ancients, and even that it is the clearest expression of the ancients' understanding of the ascetical life. In the hermit life we can most easily rediscover the essential fundamental principle of all the Christian asceticism of the ancient world. So, the present study tries to show that, far from being a deviation from authentic Christian asceticism, the hermit life in fact constitutes its most genuine, its most perfect, and, we might say, its most normative expression. It is in that sense that we call the hermit the ideal ascetic, since the hermit's life is the most perfect realization of separation from the world, which is the principal foundation of the ascetical life. This principle still retains its validity, entire and whole, in our own age, just as it did in antiquity, in every form of ascetical life, and would do so even if the hermit ideal were no longer practicable and if there were no souls called to live it out.

Once that has been established, it will be easier to speak of other forms of ascetical life, which carry through the same underlying principle, albeit in different ways and less emphatically.

So, after having analysed the essence of asceticism and its principal forms, we will have to study the imitation of Christ, its dogmatic foundation. This chapter, therefore, will set out the theological basis of the Christian ascetical ideal, and thus pointing out the way the ascetic must follow.

The following chapters will look at the ascetic ideal from two aspects on which antiquity was fond of dwelling: the ascetic as martyr, and the ascetic as soldier of Jesus Christ. These two viewpoints spring from the fundamental principle already enunciated earlier, namely that the ascetic, in separating from the world and doing battle with natural inclinations, undergoes martyrdom and does battle with the enemies of Jesus Christ and the Kingdom of Heaven. The ascetic separates from the world to follow Jesus Christ but does not do so with a purely negative goal; rather, he prefers to see his decision in a positive light, as the return to the Father with Christ. Through his life of prayer, the ascetic brings about this positive aspect, entry into the heavenly Homeland and constantly growing union with God; silence is a necessary condition for this, already implicit in separation from the world.

In dealing with the life of prayer, our study will touch on matters which we have treated more extensively in our *Théologie de la Mystique*.[3] Here we will lay more emphasis on ascetical practices insofar as they are linked with the life of prayer. Finally, since the life of prayer, like all personal piety, needs to be founded on the liturgy, it seemed useful to speak of the relationships which unite them, and so to show how to achieve a real harmony between these two essential points, which are so important for the healthy development of the ascetic's interior life.

A separate chapter has been devoted to an ascetical practice which was greatly held in honour among the ancients, the reading of Holy Scripture. It is true that nowadays it is still encouraged, but it no longer has the influence which it can and should have in the exercise of the ascetic life. That is why it seemed necessary to us to give an account of the reasons which vindicate frequent, if not continual, meditation of the Scriptures.

Our final chapter deals with the ascetic's apostolic activity, as an ascetic, and quite apart from whatever duties may be his as a priest, if he is so. These considerations represent a final endorsement of what has been said of the essence of the ascetic life.

It might be that what we are offering may seem too negative, since it is fair to say that we lay considerable emphasis on this aspect of asceticism: the necessity for detachment, mortification, and so on; however, it is not less true that the ascetic life has

---

[3] *The Doctrine of Spiritual Perfection*, by Rev. Anselm Stolz, O. S. B., Translated by Rev. Aidan Williams, O. S. B., S. T. D., Monk of Belmont Abbey, Hereford, England. B. Herder Book Co., St. Louis, MO, and London, 1938

Preface to the French Edition

its positive side, since it aims at union with God and is in some sense an anticipation of Beatitude. St Scholastica conversed with her brother St Benedict on these heavenly joys, *caelestis vitae gaudia*, during their last meeting together. We say a little of this in our chapter on the life of prayer, and have developed it extensively in our *Théologie de la Mystique*, to which we have now joined this modest work, as a first step towards a theology of asceticism.

INTRODUCTION

It is with great pleasure that I greet the translation into English of *L'Ascèse chrétienne*, the last book written by the Benedictine theologian Dom Anselm Stolz, in the fullness of his human and intellectual maturity, not long before his premature death, caused, in October 1942, by the typhus fever which he contracted from serving people affected by it.

The volume the reader has in his hands, masterfully translated by Dom Giles Conacher O. S. B., who has under his belt a more than thirty-year-long activity as translator, is a companion-piece to Stolz's *Theology of Mysticism*. Although less known than the latter, in *L'Ascèse chrétienne* Stolz's attempt at constructing a "theology of asceticism" has an undeniable importance on account of the method by which he conducted his research on Christian asceticism, *viz.* by basing it on Holy Scripture and on Patristic and Monastic literature.

In this way, Stolz contributed to help Catholic theology move forward from its monocular approach, represented by the then over-dominant Neo-Scholasticism, in which it had been strait-jacketed because of the Modernist crisis. In *L'Ascèse chrétienne* Stolz offers, in line with his other works, a balanced synthesis of Tradition and renewal, and in so doing he comes close to the programme of the *ressourcement* movement, which was enhancing a return to the biblical and patristic sources of theological tradition.

Equally important in Stolz's theological works are his spiritual freedom and openness to God's grace, two characteristics which allowed his research never to be detached from the spiritual life of the believer. Stolz himself, in the foreword to his book, is at pains to tell his readers that despite the fact that some of the ideals pursued by ascetic life may seem too high and unattainable (*e.g., eremitism*), what is asked of them is to comprehend the essential principles, both theological and spiritual, that are at the root of Christian and ascetic life.

While thanking Dom Giles for the excellent translation of Stolz's *L'Ascèse chrétienne*, I wish the readers of this book — as was intended by the Author himself — that they may draw further inspiration for living with inner freedom and joy the *sequela Christi* and his Gospel.

✠ Donato Ogliari OSB
Archabbot and Ordinary of Montecassino

FOREWORD
The lectio brevis *of Dom Anselm Stolz OSB*
ROBERTO FERRARI OSB

IT IS WITH GREAT PLEASURE THAT I greet this first edition in English, prepared by Dom Giles Conacher of Pluscarden Abbey, of *L'Ascèse chrétienne* by Fr Anselm Stolz, monk of Gerleve. Over the course of the years, interest in this book has been kept alive by various scholars and by those who still follow the ascetic life: religious and diocesan hermits. At last, the absence of an English language version of the book has been remedied! It is to be hoped that this new publication will be received with both spiritual reverence and intellectual attention, and with lively academic engagement, all of which taken together may lead to a re-discovery of the thought of Stolz about the ascetical life and the practice of the hermit life. Monastic theology needs this important complement.

When on 2 November each year, I visit the Roman cemetery of Campo Verano, burial place of the monks of the Benedictine Collegio Sant'Anselmo, I linger over the name of Anselm Stolz, in happy remembrance of that young monk (1900–1942) whose birthday, 28 January, was the same as mine. His monastery was the Abbey of Gerleve in Westphalia in Germany and he was professor of dogmatic theology at the Athenaeum of Sant'Anselmo in the years 1928–1942. He is someone I have studied at length through the primary sources, thanks to the doctoral thesis of Elmar Salmann, but above all, indirectly — through the appreciative works of Fr Benedetto Calati and through the disagreements Stolz himself had with both the Dominican and Jesuit approaches, and with the Carmelites who responded to his views with both suspicion and admiration.

Jean Leclercq writes as follows[4]:

---

[4] "Silenzio e parola nella mistica Cristiana di ieri e oggi" in Mistica e misticismo oggi. Settimana di studio di Lucca, 8–13 September 1978, Passionisti, CIPI, Roma, 1979, 61–73. French version, "Silence et parole dans l'expérience spirituelle d'hier et aujourd'hui" by Jean Leclercq OSB,

The experience of the presence of God to oneself and of oneself to God tends to appear in two ways, which correspond to the two inseparable aspects of the one and the same charity: speaking to God, and speaking of God to others. First of all to express oneself and to express God to oneself before God and for God: to exist for him is to enter into a dialogue with him, whence flows, more or less in accordance with the charism and ministry of each, the fact of saying something about him to others. Between silence and word, experience and expression there is a link; these two activities do not necessarily follow one another. They can be given one within the other and the one by means of the other. So it was that during his spiritual colloquy with the deacon Servandus that St Benedict received the vision of the Creator and of all creation.[5] In every case, the words said to men must proceed from those heard from God: they must surge up from that intimate contact with him represented by silence. But just as silence has brought into communion with the Universal, the word which overflows from it is a response to that need for communion which is expressed in communication.

It would be seriously harmful if, as a result of speaking of silence, one were to forget that word and silence are at the service of the only charism which guarantees, without illusion, the presence of God: charity.

This view of Leclercq is readily applicable to the book that we are now introducing, *Christian Asceticism*.

While the descriptive method of Poulain, who sought to place and describe the phenomenon of mysticism within a primarily *psychological* framework, was for Stolz not fully adequate, nor, equally, was the *dogmatic* approach of Garrigou-Lagrange, of whom Stolz had been a student for various courses at the *Angelicum*, fully satisfactory for Stolz, because the French Dominican gave inadequate attention to theological anthropology, ecclesiology and soteriology. It was thus that P. Anselm

---

in *Collectanea Cisterciensia*, Tome 45-1983-3, pp. 185-198.
5 *Dial.*, II, 35

Foreword

Stolz took a somewhat solitary path — at least for that historical period — basing himself on the Pauline writings, particularly 2 Cor. 12:1–5, and the Greek and Latin patristic tradition, especially in its monastic form which saw in the key theme of the *Return to Paradise* — that is, to the original Adamic friendship with God — the mystical union itself, because this union belongs to the perfection of the Christian life and to the full development of the grace of justification. This approach was typically monastic, and especially oriental-Byzantine in tone. Here Stolz revealed a glimpse of the doctrine of *the universal call to holiness* that would be more fully adopted by Vatican II, and thus of the mystical union with the Triune God which is simply the common call of all the baptized. For man the sinner, the approach to the *visio beatifica*, the beatific vision, must pass through a period of asceticism, the purifying fire of good works and *theresis* or *watchfulness*, with regard to the capital vices and the passions that deface the image and likeness of God in us, both here and now, and after death. All Christians, in fact, participate in the redemptive work of Christ and are called to the restoration of Paradise Lost and to the direct vision of God, bringing justifying grace to completion in us and arriving at mystical union; when this is not achieved in this life, the further purification of purgatory will lead to the completion of this mystical participation.

This mystical union with God in the economy of salvation is realized through Christ. It is communion with Christ and with His mysteries that is the deepest foundation of this mysticism; the same would be said by Odo Casel of the school of the Abbey of Maria Laach, where Stolz received his own philosophical formation. We are dealing with a union that begins with the sacrament of baptism but which only finds its full completion in the Eucharist. Mystical grace transcends sacramental order, and it gratuitously gives to the Christian an experience of the supernatural life.

In *Christian Asceticism* (1939), Stolz does not claim to offer a manual of ascetical doctrine: rather he seeks to cast a fuller light on a few points, a teaching which is a synthetic summary of the essentials for the solitary life, drawn from the patristic-monastic tradition. In fact, the origins of the book lie in a series of conferences given at Chevetogne in 1939, brought together in this volume. The author starts by immediately asking what state of life most effectively and easily leads to perfection. His answer is the eremitical life, the life of the hermit. In fact, living in solitude is the aim and summit of all sanctity; all other forms of the spiritual life are but steps leading to this point, even the cenobitic or community life of monks is only a preparation for it. Expressed in theological terms, the eremitical life is a following of Christ, a martyrdom, a battle with Christ against Satan.

Let us briefly consider the structure of the book:

1. Preface
2. The hermit
3. Other forms of ascetical life
4. The imitation of Jesus Christ
5. The ascetic as martyr
6. The soldier of Jesus Christ
7. Silence
8. The life of prayer
9. Liturgy and personal devotion
10. Sacred Scripture
11. The ascetic as apostle
12. Epilogue

The important instruments of the ascetical life are silence, liturgical prayer, personal prayer, Scripture reading (*lectio divina*), but also the apostolate, not in the priestly sense of the cure of souls, but rather in that sense which is typical of the hermit and of the monk, the sense of spiritual paternity. Stolz, for all that he is focused is on monastic asceticism, does not forget Christians who live in the world: in fact, this ascetical ideal is in truth valid for all Christians; the differences are only in the circumstances and in the ways of living it out. It is in the most extreme form of the ascetical life (the eremitical) that the essence of asceticism appears most clearly: separating oneself from the world so as to give oneself to God with the greatest freedom possible. Clearly this is not to say that all Christians must lead the eremitical life, for that is a particular calling. Stolz puts forward both the *negative* aspects of the ascetical life, mortification and separation from the world, and the *positive*, its

Foreword

focus on union with God and the way, in which, in a manner of speaking, it anticipates the life of blessedness.[6]

Thus at the beginning of the twentieth century a debate opened on the nature of mysticism, of prayer and of contemplation. Let us take a brief look at the protagonists:

Augustin Poulain SJ	Mysticism derives from evidence drawn from experience and is essentially different from the ordinary way of prayer.	R. de Maumigny SJ; K. Richstätter SJ; M. de la Taille.
Auguste Saudreau	Mysticism is interpreted starting from dogmatic theology; there are various steps in the ordinary life of grace. He holds that there is a common vocation to the mystical life.	E. Dimmler; J. Zahn; E. Krebs.
Alois Mager OSB	Like Poulain, he starts from a systematic observation of mystical experiences; but he argues that while *psychologically* ordinary prayer and mystical prayer are essentially different, from a *theological* point of view, the opposite is true, they differ only in their grade.	
Réginald Garrigou-Lagrange OP	He approaches the question from the perspective of dogmatic-speculative theology and accepts that there is a difference in kind between ordinary and mystical prayer, a direct result of the gifts of the Holy Spirit. He is however convinced that all Christians are called to mystical prayer, the heart of which is infused contemplation: such prayer is the authentic and definitive development of sanctifying grace.	

---

6 "Stolz", *Dictionnaire de Spiritualité*, XIV, 1252–1257 (Beauchesne, Paris, 1937–1995)

Anselm Stolz OSB	While following Garrigou-Lagrange's line, he puts the emphasis on the theological principles particular to mysticism. His mystical theology is marked by the importance he gives to the Fathers (particularly to the Greek Fathers) rather than to a strict attention to scholastic theology; he uses the concept of "trans-psychological experience"; he tends to undervalue the Spanish mystics of the Sixteenth Century; he is open to further theological discussion, re-affirming the theological integrity of the patristic period in which asceticism, liturgy, spirituality and doctrine formed a whole, a *unicum*. Fundamentally, Stolz makes an important contribution to a vision of the mystical life which is dogmatically based.	J. de Guilbert SJ; Hans Urs von Balthasar; K. Rahner SJ; A. Brunner; H. de Lubac SJ; J. Leclercq OSB

In concluding this theological summary of *Christian Asceticism*, I would like to recall how the Carmelites (we can think of the French *Études Carmélitaines*, and also of Fr Gabriele of S. Maria Maddalena OCD), while not denying the truly theological aspect of asceticism and mysticism, underlined the importance in them of psychology; developing a spiritual theology thus requires a theological method that is both deductive, given the type of discipline it is, but which also must not neglect the descriptive and inductive approaches appropriate to the experimental sciences.

It is in the context of this shared understanding, in which all scholars accepted a compromise between a spiritual, theologico-psychological science and a deductive and inductive methodology, that we find the contribution of Anselm Stolz, so markedly open to the theological aspects of asceticism and of mysticism in particular. The polemics with Fr Gabriele of S. Maria Maddalena immediately forced the discussion to limit itself to the

Foreword

question of the psychological character of spiritual theology; the responses which developed about the "*trans*-psychological" if not the "*a*-psychological" characteristics of the action of grace, favoured this limitation.[7] The controversial aspects of all this,

---

[7] The debate on the relationship between psychology and the theology of mysticism began with the publication of Stolz's book Theologie der Mystik (Pustet, Regensburg, 1936). The work was translated into three languages: English, *The Doctrine of Spiritual Perfection* (St Louis, MO,. Herder, London, 1938); French, *Théologie de la mystique* (Chevetogne, Bénédictins d'Amay, 1939); and Italian, Teologia della mistica (Morcelliana, Brescia, 1940, ed. Dom Matronola). It was based on the course given by the author at Salzburg during the University Weeks of August 1935 on the theme "The Dogmatic Foundations of Mysticism"; during the same Weeks, Dom A. Mager OSB gave a course on "The Psychological Foundations of Mysticism". This fact explains the apparent "one-sidedness" of Stolz's book, and these circumstances were unfortunately not brought to the attention of the reader in the Author's Preface, in which he wrote only of his own contribution. The title subsequently chosen for the publication did not give the impression that he was dealing only with one aspect, given that the word Theology has of itself a broader sense, including questions of practical import. This is the explanation of why the negative reactions to the book from A. Winkelhofer, M. T-L Penido and L. Cerfaux were so vigorous. Above all, there was an exchange of articles between Penido and Stolz. The famous address of Fr Gabriele di S. Maria Maddalena OCD to the Roman Academy of St Thomas, entitled "The Psychological Character of Spiritual Theology" (1940) further stimulated the discussion, causing Fr Garrigou-Lagrange OP, member of the same Academy, to develop the question, showing great appreciation for the Stolz-Penido debate. Fr Colosio was unfavorable to Stolz's views as he understood them; in Vita Cristiana (1940), he forcefully emphasized the divergence between the two currents, one psychological and the other realist. The same edition of that review included an important article by Stolz, "Mistica e Psicologia," in which he explained that he had limited his own researches to the dogmatic foundations of mysticism, thus deliberately excluding from his study the psychological aspects which he nonetheless fully recognized as perfectly legitimate, and thus he chose as the title of his book, *The Theology of Mysticism*. One can thus make a distinction between the Theology of Mysticism and Mystical Theology. The latter refers to the supernatural knowledge itself, the former to the explanation of such knowledge. In the same review, Fr Gabriele of SMM responded: it seemed arbitrary to him to restrict theology of mysticism exclusively to the search for the dogmatic foundations of mysticism, precisely because Theology has other tasks, for example, that of guiding the mystical soul. In response to this

much studied today, requires a reassessment, with an eye to a more complete integration.

May the present volume enkindle in those who read it just such a dynamic integration of the intellectual and the affective.

> Roberto Ferrari OSB
> *Benedictine monk,*
> *Academic assistant to Fr Luigi Borriello OCD,*
> *Researcher in Mystical and Monastic*
> *Spiritual Theology, Naples;*
> *STL in Spiritual Theology, Monastic,*
> *Pontifical Athenaeum of Sant'Anselmo,Rome.*
> *Curia Generalizia of the Subiaco-Cassinese*
> *Benedictine Congregation, Rome.*

---

observation, Stolz sent a letter and then went to see Fr Gabriele personally. They agreed to publish an article together in "Vita Cristiana" in which the two theologians would show that, leaving aside the question of terminology, their two approaches were complementary. The premature death of our monk (19 October 1942) prevented this. We can however note with certainty, that already in 1940, an article of Ceriani in Scuola Cattolica showed that the two points of view needed to be reconciled.

CHAPTER I

The Hermit Life

NEVER IN THE COURSE OF HER HIStory has the Church claimed to lay down a directive, or imposed a single way of life, upon all those who, impelled by the need for greater perfection, sought an ascetic life. Today, as yesterday, you can meet ascetics and saints in all walks of life, in every social class, in the most varied states of life, in married life, in the cloister and in solitude.

All the same, it is not without importance to find out what state, what form of life, the ascetic tends to choose in quest of holiness. Moreover, we can and must admit that among the different kinds of life, there is, objectively speaking, one which is the most perfect. This does not mean to say that every ascetic should necessarily adopt the kind of life which is, "in itself", the most perfect, and that to act otherwise would show pusillanimity and weakness; God's call must be taken into consideration. God does not demand that all Christians be cast from the same mould, but he does wish them to be perfect in their situation and in the way of life that fits their personality best. What confers Christian perfection on a man is not his state in life; we are not dealing with a sacrament, which has its effect by the simple performance of the action, *ex opere operato*, to use the time-honoured phrase. Let us not forget that the intimate life of grace, which is exteriorized in the various states, is so rich and inexhaustible that it cannot be limited to a single formula. This is why the different forms of the ascetic life are admissible, because each can lead to perfection. The one we hold to be objectively the most perfect simply shows, more than the others, what constitutes Christian holiness; one could say that it makes easier the climb to the highest summits of perfection.

A detailed examination of the different forms of ascetic life offers more than mere anecdotal and historical interest; apart from the practical usefulness that one who wishes to choose the way which fits best may find, this examination is intended to demonstrate the various expressions of Christian perfection, and so to uncover the treasure hidden within them. That is why a theology of Christian ascesis cannot afford to neglect any of its forms. Its chief object is to bring out their common source, the very principle of the religious life whence these different aspects spring.

This subject gains further interest if we give thought to the differing conceptions of the ascetic and monastic life which are among the many characteristics which distinguish the Western and Eastern Churches. Among our nations, the cenobitic ideal still enjoys an unrivalled favour, while in the East the ancient attraction of the hermit life is still very much alive, as is shown by the considerable number of anchorites. Coming to a clearer understanding of the goals sought by the cenobitic and the eremitic lives will contribute to a better understanding of the spirit of each of these Churches.

We meet the first signs of the ascetic life in the Acts of the Apostles: some Christians trying to practise the Lord's commands and counsels as perfectly as possible, so as to be better prepared to meet him on the day of his triumphant return. This is what St Paul has in mind, when he tells the Corinthians, "To the unmarried and widows I say that it is well for them to remain single as I am" (1 Cor. 7:8). The Apostle thus thinks that celibacy and widowhood are preferable to marriage, despite the latter's legitimacy and the fact that it has been raised to the dignity of a sacrament. The reason for this is clearly that these states allow an easier concentration on the things of the Lord, because free from other concerns; the Apostle says as much: "I want you to be free from anxieties. The unmarried man is anxious about the affairs of the Lord, how to please the Lord.... The unmarried woman or girl is anxious about the affairs of the Lord" (1 Cor. 7:32, 34). He offers this advice to the widow, "If the husband dies, [the wife] is free to be married to whom she wishes, only in the Lord. But in my judgement, she is more blessed if she remains as she is. And I think that I have the Spirit of God" (1 Cor. 7:39–40).

So here we see, apart from the life of Jesus and the apostolic life of his disciples, the primitive form of the ascetic life. This glimpse of the life of the first Christian communities makes it easier to see the similarities and the differences, when we compare this with the ascetic tendency which later developed in the Church. We find in the heart of the community, Christians who, without separating themselves from their fellows, were living a lifestyle which was stranger to the ways of the world, entirely given to the quest for the things of heaven.

St Paul insists that devoting oneself to such a way of life is a matter of complete freedom. He states that it depends above all on the grace of the Lord, and not on our will alone: "Each has his own special gift from God, one of one kind and one of another" (1 Cor. 7:7). Since the sources are silent on the matter, we cannot, without indulging in guesswork and theories, say more about how these Christians lived. Another New Testament passage shows devotees of the ascetic life endowed with a special charism: the Acts of the Apostles cites the case of the deacon Phillip, who had, "four unmarried daughters who prophesied" (Acts 21:9), which shows that ascetics shared in the most important activities of community life, and that they were sometimes chosen by the Holy Spirit as instruments to discharge the greatest responsibilities in the Church. In apostolic times, the prophets were those who, under the impulse of the Holy Spirit, made clear the intentions of Providence and, equally inspired, explained obscure matters of Gospel teaching.

St John's Apocalypse leads us to think that the number of ascetics was already considerable. It suggests that they enjoyed great esteem in the primitive Church, since they alone, who have remained virgin for love of Christ, are promised a special reward. They alone can sing, "a new song before the throne ... and no one could learn that song, except the one hundred and forty-four thousand.... It is these who have not defiled themselves with women, for they are chaste; it is these who follow the Lamb wherever he goes" (Apoc 14:3-4).

So, from the Church's very origins, people in the heart of the Christian community practised some sort of ascetic life, with the hope of attaining to the first place in eternal life, and sharing the heavenly liturgy around the throne of the Lamb. These acetic members of the Christian community will be met with still more frequently in later ages.

When Origen writes — as he often does — of Christian perfection and the means to attain it, he does so under the influence of Neo-Platonic philosophy. Even so, his ideas were widely influential in the Church, and still today his fundamental teachings are universally accepted. According to him, the ascetic life leads to contemplation, and all ascetic practice is secondary to that goal. Contemplation leads to union with God, the spiritual Being attainable by the spirit, and draws on towards divinisation.

The idea that contemplation is the basis of union with God, and that this in turn is a condition of divinisation, is a view widely current in Catholic tradition. St Irenaeus wrote, "He shares in divine life, who sees God."[1]

According to Origen, this process of divinisation only occurs gradually. We do not acquire perfection instantaneously. In order to arrive at the goal, a sustained effort is required, passing through different stages. The ascetic means which Origen most frequently recommended (because they were the most effective), were fasting, prayer and the study of Holy Scripture.

The specific object of these means was separation of the ascetics from the world and fleshly desire, in order to allow them to devote themselves, unhindered, to spiritual and divine things. We also find in Origen an allusion to a further means: absolute separation from the world. The interpretation of the text which follows is debated; it runs like this: "If one wishes to serve God, one must separate from the world. It is necessary to abandon the world, I do not mean materially, but spiritually; we do not progress with our feet, but by faith."[2] Some people claim that Origen here was taking issue with the hermits, who separated themselves not merely spiritually, but materially, withdrawing into the desert, and that he thought that it was their duty to remain within the Christian community, practising a merely spiritual separation. If this were the case, then this passage from Origen would be in line with what later became almost universal

---

1 Irenaeus, *Adv. Haer.*, 4, 38, 3: *Five Books of S. Irenaeus — Against Heresies*, trans. Rev. John Keble, M.A, Other Works (James Parker & Co., Oxford, Rivingtons, London, 1872), p. 438.
2 Origen, *Hom. In Exod.*, 3:3; *Origen, Homilies on Genesis and Exodus*, translated by Ronald E. Heine, FOTC Vol. 71 (CUA Press, 1982), p. 253.

among Christian ascetics, a tendency to abandon the society of men in order to go and dwell in desert places. Nonetheless, the following interpretation seems preferable, that Origen is aware of the ascetic value of a total separation from the world; he recognizes it, and that is why he rightly insists on the truth that it is not physical distance alone, but above all spiritual separation which favours perfection. The first of these means is subordinate to the second, and ensures its effectiveness.

In the fourth century, the eremitic ideal undoubtedly prevailed. As a general rule, the ascetic no longer lived amidst the community, but separated from it and went off into the desert, to share the life of some few companions. Some even withdrew for many years into inaccessible places, and refused all contact, however harmless, with their fellows.

What was the origin of this triumph of the hermit life? Some theories, fashionable at the beginning of the twentieth century, claimed that non-Christian religious influences gave birth to eremitical life. They are no longer in favour, and it is admitted that monastic life, and in particular its eremitical form, are natural consequences of the Christian concept of perfection. But how are we to make sense of this extraordinary phenomenon? Why did ascetics, who up to then had been members of the Christian community, its nucleus and most solid rampart in persecutions, decide to abandon their brothers and sisters and withdraw into the desert? Because these were not isolated cases, it involved great crowds of the faithful, as though it were the most natural thing in the world, with no one raising the slightest question about its legitimacy. It is true that the persecutions in the preceding period would only exceptionally have permitted such separations, when the ascetics' charitable work was needed by Christian society. Later on, when the hermit life was in full flower, the hermits often returned to their communities if a persecution broke out, in order to strengthen the faithful and take the chance to confess their faith publicly. The early Christian belief in the imminent end of the world also had an enduring limiting influence on the eremitical ideal. As we have just seen, the persecutions cannot furnish the final or deepest reason for the movement, because, far from providing an overall explanation, they are only valid in a few isolated cases. Something so novel and so abruptly contrasting with previous practice can only be explained by causes stemming from the very idea of Christian perfection itself.

The same must be said of the economic difficulties that might have led some to withdraw into the desert; they might have provided the immediate excuse, but not the real cause of such a large-scale movement. Still less tenable is the suggestion that the moral weakness of certain Christians, unable to cope with the difficulties and temptations of life in the world, might have led them to withdraw into solitude, where they could comfortably practise the Christian virtues, for it is well known that hermit life demands a moral strength well beyond that required by life in the world.

More recent authors have sometimes spoken of a "secularisation of Christianity" in the fourth and fifth centuries. They maintain that, once the era of persecutions was over, professing Christianity was no longer dangerous when it had become the state religion; rather, it opened avenues to advancement. The masses entered the Church, and its authorities had to come to agreement with the civil power. This gave rise to a sort of compromise between Christianity, which up till then had been so austere, and public life, integrated with paganism and Christianity's absolute antithesis. According to these authors, this secularisation of Christianity was the chief reason for the more fervent Christians' withdrawal, in order to maintain their primitive austerity. Even Nikolai Arseniew, in his most interesting study on Eastern monachism, seems to incline towards this view:

> While Christianity lived under the threat of martyrdom, there was no sign of the danger of secularization.... But when peace came, once the life of the world found a footing in the Church, once Christianity was declared the State religion, then many began to flee the world into which, by contrast, the Church was making its way, a world unregenerate, still attached to its old habits and way of life.[3]

---

3 N. Arseniew, *Das Mönchtum und der asketisch-mystisch Weg in der Ostkirche*, in *Der Christliche Osten*, 1939, p. 172.

The Hermit Life

However, as a principal factor, the "secularization of Christianity" cannot account for a new form of ascetic life, especially on such a broad scale. As we said earlier, the reasons are to be sought in intrinsic causes, which led to the appearance of the hermit life as the summit of perfection, and the logical consequence of existing ascetic practice.

In our opinion, there were three reasons which led the ascetics to leave the world and withdraw into the desert. Above all was the ascetics' conviction that if they wanted to be perfect, they must separate themselves from the world as much as possible. Secondly, they were convinced that they must, in a quite special way, do battle with the devil, enemy of mankind and of the Christian in particular—that they must confront him openly, and do so in solitude. Finally, there was the idea, very current at that time, that the ascetic, like everyone else, had lost Paradise through sin, and that he must go in search of it, because there alone is our real homeland.

In putting forward these three theological foundations of the hermit life, we are not trying to claim that they were involved in the vocation of each individual hermit, nor that one should bear them constantly in mind in the history of the hermit life; we simply wish to demonstrate by their means that the eremitical life was a logical consequence which naturally followed from an ascetic life based on the most authentic elements of Christian teaching. Further, we affirm that these reasons indeed contributed to the extraordinary development of this way of life, and that the ascetics referred to one or other of these reasons to justify their way of acting, as monastic antiquity bears witness.

* * *

The idea that Christians should make themselves strangers to "this world" forms a part of the most authentic bedrock of Christian thought. The Lord himself told his disciples, "the world has hated them because they do not belong to the world" (Jn. 17:14). Nothing could be more natural, since the Christian, a member of Jesus Christ, citizen of the Kingdom of God, cannot belong to the kingdom of the devil, who has pitched his tents in this sin-filled world. This is why Origen, as we have already pointed out, imposes on the ascetic a complete separation, which must be primarily spiritual, from the world. Tertullian, whose lively temperament tended to carry him away, expressed this thought in forceful terms which have the fortunate result of bringing out the underlying idea: "For the Christian in this world, the most urgent thing to do, is to leave it as soon as possible."[4] St Augustine expressed himself with more restraint,

> Christ said, "I do not pray for this world, but for those the Father has given me." The very fact that they had been given him by the Father, meant that they no longer belonged to the world for which the Redeemer did not pray.[5]

The Sayings of the Fathers tell a story which is a good illustration of this: A Palace official called Arsenius one day prayed to God like this, "Lord, show me the way to salvation." Then he heard a voice which replied, "Arsenius, flee men and you will be saved." Arsenius obeyed the command and withdrew into the desert, since this seemed to him to correspond most closely with the advice he had been given. He had already been living in the desert as a hermit for some time, when one day he prayed the same prayer to God. The voice which he recognized replied, "Arsenius, take flight, keep silence and keep your soul in peace; these three things will free you from sin." By this and other examples, the lives of the ancient Fathers demonstrate that separation from the world and flight from men were considered an effective means of escaping from occasions of sin.

The aim of their flight was solitude in the desert. It was thus that they sought, by a complete gift of themselves to God, truly to separate themselves from the world. The *Apophthegms* say Abba Andrew put it like this, "Three things are fitting for monks: leaving your native land, living in poverty and exercising patience in silence." It is clear that the hermit life was seen as the logical perfection of one of the basic principles of the ascetic life and Christian life in general: separation from the world.

---

4 Tertullian, *Apologeticus* 41
5 Augustine, *On John* 107, I: *Tractates on the Gospel of John, 55–11*, trans. John W. Rettig, FOTC 90 (CUA Press 1994), p. 273.

The Hermit Life

That should not lead us to conclude that every Christian, or even every ascetic, should practise this form of life. We all have to separate ourselves from the world, or, to put it better, we are all, by the fact of our incorporation into Christ, separated from the world, and if we are logical about it, we have to put this separation into practice in daily life. We are not all, however, expected to reach such heights as the hermit; that requires a special vocation. But it is nonetheless still true, and this is what interests us, that in this perspective one can see the life of the anchorite as a form of Christian ascetic life, and even regard it as the highest degree of ascesis which human effort can reach with the living support of grace.

* * *

In order to form a correct picture of the Christian life, we need to add the idea of detachment from the world, the no less essential element of struggle with the demon. St Paul alludes to this when he speaks of the weapons which the Christian must take up; he says,

> Put on the whole armour of God, that you may be able to stand against the wiles of the devil. For we are not contending against flesh and blood, but against the principalities, against the powers, against the world rulers of this present darkness, against the spiritual hosts of wickedness in the heavenly places. Therefore take the whole armour of God, that you may be able to withstand in the evil day, and having done all, to stand (Eph. 6:11–13).

In truth, the idea of armour is only a variation on the theme of that other well-known image, which portrays sanctifying grace as a garment covering the nakedness of our nature, giving it a brilliance and a splendour far beyond its ordinary condition. In heaven this garment will be glorious and luminous like the garment of the angel beside the Lord's tomb, or like the Lord's on Mount Tabor, with Moses and Elijah (Mt. 17:1–9), symbolic of heavenly purity, and of the soul united to God. In heaven, where peace reigns eternally, weapons and struggle will have no place. Here below, in contrast, supernatural progress requires our battling, constant struggle to defend our supernatural treasures against the enemy's ambushes and attacks. That is why the state of grace on this earth is not only compared to a garment, but to armour, too. This is the state of all Christians, by virtue of their membership of the Church. The "I promise" of baptism takes the Christian from Satan's hordes to the holy soldiery of Jesus Christ.

If we must think of every Christian as a combatant, then even more so must this be true of the monk, since he seeks to live out in his own life the highest Christian ideal. In the Prologue to his Rule, St Benedict calls upon his generosity, inviting the candidate who wishes to fight under Christ's standard, to do battle with the powerful and glorious weapons of obedience. Cenobites, as he puts it, are monks who perform their military service under a rule and an Abbot; whereas hermits, as St Benedict might have said in modern terms, are the special forces; they have already been trained, amid the ranks of the cenobites, to do battle with the devil, and are not afraid alone to confront the enemy in the desert. So, the Christian life, and still more so the monk's, and much more so that of the hermit, is a struggle against the devil. In the combat against Satan, the hermit belongs among the champions and the specialists. It is very much to the point that St Benedict speaks of their "single combat", for the profound reason that the hermit goes and seeks out the devil in his hidden lairs. Holy Scripture teaches us that the desert is the territory where the demon dwells, the region of the earth where his writ runs. "When the unclean spirit has gone out of a man, he passes through waterless places, seeking rest" (Lk. 11:24). The Evangelist also tells us that a man, who had been possessed for many years had been driven out into the desert (Lk. 8:29). When St Antony withdrew into solitude, the demons complained, trying to maintain their rights: "Leave our domain, what are you doing in the desert?" Seeing that St Antony's example was followed by others, they groaned and said, "There's nowhere left for us.... There are Christians everywhere, and even the desert is full of monks."

The anchorites well knew that in going to the desert they were entering the very territory of the demons, and they did

The Hermit Life

so deliberately so as to battle them more effectively, hand to hand. Cassian, the most authoritative spokesman for the views of the ancient monks, said, "In their desire to battle the demons openly and directly, they did not fear to go out into the vast solitudes of the desert."[6]

Karl Holl, whose analysis of certain aspects of ancient monasticism is very penetrating, says of St Antony,

> When the enemy had been pointed out to him, St Antony felt the need to go and confront him by force in his own lair." Then he adds an explanatory note, "Only he who has attained a certain degree of perfection is called to face up to the demons in this way, for only he is capable of seeing them.[7]

This second aspect of the Christian life, which every Christian can and must to some extent embody, is further testimony to the fact that the hermit life is the logical and almost necessary consequence of a Christian life lived to the full, in its highest and most perfect form.

* * *

Now we come to the third point. The theological theories of the earliest Fathers continually and insistently emphasize that we must win back our first perfection and go in search of the Paradise we lost by sin, and this to such an extent that from this idea flows their definition of man. "It gives God great joy," says Origen, "to see you live in this world as though in a tent, that your heart and soul are not rooted in it, and that you do not sigh for possession of earthly goods, and that you are not tied to this passing life as though it was something enduring; in

---

6   Cassian, Coll. 18, 6, 2, p. 639; Coll. 7, 23, 2, p. 263; *John Cassian: The Conferences*. Translated and annotated by Boniface Ramsey, O. P. (Paulist Press, NY 1996; ACW no. 57). Elsewhere he tells of the new state of affairs brought about by the influx of monks into the desert, "Virtute crucis etiam deserta penetrante et ubique ejus gratia coruscante, retusa est nequitia daemonum": "Penetrating even the deserts with the power of the cross, and with its grace shining out everywhere, the wickedness of the demons was blunted"; Coll. 7, 23, 2–p. 263.

7   K. Holl, *Enthusiasmus und Bussgewalt* (Leipzig, 1898), p. 145

other words, that you are hastening towards your true homeland, from which, alas, you were separated, and that you say, 'Here I am a guest and a pilgrim like my Fathers'."[8] To this idea of pilgrimage, Origen adds that of exile: we have been driven from Paradise, and so are poor exiles, but the goal of our wandering life is our lost homeland. Speaking to the newly baptized, St Cyril of Jerusalem said, "If you break with the devil, if you break the bonds that chain you to him, if you tear up the ancient treaties made with Hell, then the Paradise of God which was planted in the East will be open to you."[9]

The idea of a return to a lost Paradise became part of the ordinary expression of the patrimony of Christian thought from the earliest centuries, so it is no surprise to find it given a triumphant welcome by the monastic world. The *Regula Magistri*, which is generally thought to be a re-write of the Rule of St Benedict,[10] does not simply, like St Benedict, speak of a return to God which monastic life should bring about, but also of an expulsion of the first man from the earthly Paradise and of a possible return to it for those redeemed by Jesus Christ. The *Regula Magistri* offers monastic ascesis as a certain means by which to recover Paradise.

"The land which is ours, is Paradise," said St Gregory the Great, speaking of the ascetic's Christian virtues.

> Having discovered Jesus Christ, we cannot return to the road by which we came. Pride, disobedience, enjoyment of earthly things, the fact that we have tasted the forbidden fruit, have led to us losing the land which was ours; tears, obedience, contempt for material things, mastery of carnal desires will lead us back to it again.[11]

---

8 Origen, *Hom. In Num.* 23, 11, 1; *Origène, Homélies sur les Nombres, III*, nouvelle édition par Louis Doutreleau, SJ, Sources chrétiennes [SC] 461 (Cerf, Paris, 2001), p. 141.
9 Cyril of Jerusalem, Mystagogical catecheses, I, 9; *The Writings of St Cyril of Jerusalem*, Vol. 2, translated by Leo P. McCauley, S. J. and Anthony A. Stephenson, FOTC Vol. 64 (CUA Press 1970), p. 158.
10 Translator's note: Nowadays the reverse is thought to be the case.
11 Gregory the Great, Gospel Homilies 10, 7. (PL 76, 1075–1312). This

The Hermit Life

If we are to have a correct understanding of the theory of hermit life and defend it, we cannot neglect this idea of the return to Paradise; indeed, we should give it more attention. According to an ancient belief, the Paradise from which our first parents were driven still exists, but in a place where we other men cannot reach. Access to this Paradise, which is surrounded by a belt of fire and separated from inhabited regions by impassable deserts, is forbidden to humans subject to sin. St Thomas himself is convinced that this is true, and so teaches.[12] Since this idea was common coin among ascetics, it is not in the least surprising that, in order to recover the Paradise of our first parents, they should have physically separated themselves from society in order to withdraw into desert places, which were viewed as an intermediate zone between the inhabited world and Paradise, and so come closer to their true native land. So one can see how this theological viewpoint, essential to the understanding of Christian life in general, and still more for understanding the ascetic life, should have impelled ascetics to the anchorite's life, and that to the extent of leading them to bury themselves in the desert solitudes.

The idea we have just described, of the return to Paradise, supplies the deepest theological explanation for the action of the ascetics who abandoned their native land and, after having wandered here and there, hid themselves in distant and desolate places. So it is no surprise to encounter allusions to this idea, some clearer than others, in ascetic literature.[13] The monk does not only detach himself from the world, but also sees himself as a traveller on his way to Paradise. He searches, convinced

---

reference agrees with the Maurist, Paris, edition of 1640, Hom. X, 26D. *Gregory the Great: Forty Gospel Homilies*, translated from the Latin by Dom David Hurst, Monk of Portsmouth Abbey (Cistercian Publications, Kalamazoo, Michigan, 1990); Cistercian Studies Series: One-Hundred-Twenty-Three, p. 59 uses a different numbering, referring to this as Homily 8.

12   Thomas Aquinas, *Summa theol.*, I, q. 102, *de loco hominis, qui est Paradisus*, The garden of Eden the scene of innocence; St Thomas Aquinas, *Summa Theologiae*, vol. 13, *Man made to God's image (1a 90–102)*, Latin text, English translation, Introduction and Glossary by Edmund Hill O. P. (Hawkesyard, Blackfriars 1963), p. 182

13   Reitzenstein, R. A. *Historia Monachorum und Historia lausiaca*, Göttingen, 1916, p. 171.

that he will find it at the end of his earthly pilgrimage. Further, divine grace will give him foretastes of Paradise, even here below, consolations which will reward his effort. So, in contemplation he will from time to time enjoy the delights of the heavenly life and will receive an anticipation, admittedly often in imperfect and transitory forms, of this or that privilege of our first parents, that the longed-for glory of final perfection will fix forever.

* * *

All this leads us to the conclusion that the hermit life is the natural conclusion, we might make bold to say, of the ascetic life. This is clear, if we consider the theological reasons which led the Christian ascetics who had thitherto been integrated into their communities to leave their families and the surroundings in which they had been living, in order to withdraw into the desert.

Further, we think we have made it clear that, in order to explain the surprising phenomenon of such a rapid development of the eremitical life and its extraordinary success, it is not enough to have recourse to purely external reasons, nor to the alleged "secularisation of the Church"; the only explanation is to be found built in to the very dynamic of Christian asceticism, taking the legitimate principles implicitly found in the Gospel teachings to their logical limits. The final conclusion reached by the hermit — separation from the world — shows us clearly what is the essence of the ascetic life: the expression, *extra mundum fieri*, "to become outside the world", does indeed seem to us the best summary of the ascetic life in general, not merely the hermit life. The ascetic, whether living in the family circle or in the church community makes every effort to achieve as great a possible detachment from the world, to that end mortifying every disordered love for creatures; if aspiring to a more complete detachment, he starts to refrain from all sorts of social activities which might divert him from his resolution. The hermit finally comes to its ultimate consequence, and digs a trench between himself and mankind, and alone with God devotes himself entirely to the contemplation of heavenly things.

* * *

The Hermit Life

Two testimonies of unquestionable authority confirm this view, St Thomas Aquinas and Pope Pius XI.

We have already stated that in the Western Church the hermit ideal has never in practice enjoyed the standing which the cenobitic life has always enjoyed. St Thomas, who belonged to the Dominicans, a cenobitic order, explicitly raised the question as to which of these two, cenobitic or eremitic life, should have pre-eminence? His conclusion is that,

> Solitude ... is not of itself perfection, but a means of arriving at perfection.... Nor is it a way of practising the active life, but rather the contemplative life.... So solitude does not suit religious orders whose goal is works of the active life. It does however suit orders founded to devote themselves to contemplation. We should, however, consider whether one who lives alone should be sufficient unto himself.... So, solitude is fitting for those who devote themselves to contemplation and have already reached perfection. But one can reach perfection by two routes: either by divine grace alone ... or gain it by the exercise of the virtues. In that exercise, men are helped in two ways by the company of people like them. First, in the matter of understanding, because in that way they may be instructed in the things to be contemplated, and secondly in matters of purity of heart, because the example and admonitions of a neighbour will correct the dangerous attachments that are inherent in human nature. Social life is therefore necessary for the exercise of perfection, while solitude, on the other hand, is suitable for those already perfect.... But in the same way as the one who is perfect is ahead of the one on the way to perfection, so the life of solitaries, taken up after suitable preparation, prevails over community life. However, engaging in such a life without first having had the required formation is very dangerous, unless divine grace has supplied what would normally have to be acquired, experience and training, as was the case for St Antony and St Benedict.[14]

---

14 Aquinas, *Summa theologiae. II, II, q. 188, a. 8, corpus; Vol. 47, The*

So St Thomas recognizes the primacy of the hermit life. All the same, he thinks that a preparation in cenobitic life is almost indispensable; because if solitude is to be a real source of profit for the spiritual life, it presupposes an already achieved considerable degree of advancement in the way of perfection. The same ideas lie behind his replies to the objections which accompany his account: these objections insist on the importance of community life for the exercise of virtue. St Thomas replies that those who have already reached perfection don't need anyone else's help. Nor do they need to obey a superior, since they are led by the Spirit of God himself. However, they possess the perfection of obedience in the *praeparatio animi*, the preparation of the soul, in the sense that if, in one way or another, they were put back into contact with men, they would be immediately disposed to obedience. Their hidden life, St Thomas goes on, is not useless to the Church, and to ask that they devote themselves instead to some task more "useful" to society would be an indication of an excessively "naturalist" mentality. Their service to society consists precisely in their unceasing prayer for their brothers and sisters, and in their example of a life closer to that of the angels than of men. To the objection which, based on man's social nature, would exclude the eremitic ideal—at least as a state of life—or would argue that it is not objectively the most perfect, St Thomas replies by following the line of the classical tradition. You can separate yourself from society for two reasons, he says: either because you can't stand life in society—which would be indicative of great imperfection, and a beastly, almost inhuman nature—or else on account of a desire to devote yourself entirely to things divine, something which cannot have other than a supernatural cause.

This reply shows clearly that in order to understand and esteem the hermit life, one must avoid giving too much importance to purely natural and rationalistic ideas, because we are here dealing with something that goes beyond nature. True, grace never destroys the natural order, which is why it remains true, even in the order of grace, that man is a social being. Even

Pastoral and Religious Lives (2a2ae. 183-9). Latin Text, English Translation, introduction and Glossary by Jordan Aumann O. P. (Chicago, Illinois. Blackfriars 1973), p. 183.

so, grace can go beyond nature and move people to resolutions and practices which, in the light of merely reasonable principles, might seem less perfect, as we see in the case we are considering.

While replying to the objections raised by the article we have summarized, St Thomas discusses the problem of the practice of the virtues in general. He shows that the hermit, or, more precisely, whoever has embraced that form of life after the required preparation by an ascetic life in community, no longer needs to work at the different virtues, because he has already attained perfection and is in such a state that he will accomplish the acts of virtue as occasion presents. The difficulty increases if we consider the case of charity, the pivotal virtue of the Christian life, from which no one may dispense himself and which all are bound to practise, since God is love (Jn. 4:16). So, if he wants to live as a true Christian, the hermit too must practise charity; indeed, as a perfect Christian, he is bound to exercise charity in a more perfect degree. His primary fulfilment of this precept will be by the contemplative life to which he has devoted himself; in it he exercises the love of God to a heroic degree, giving up all that might distract from God. But charity towards our neighbour is subordinate to love of God, and we love our neighbour out of love for God. Hence, whoever perfectly practises love of God by that very fact also satisfies the commandment of love for neighbour. The same could be said of martyrdom. One might criticize the martyrs' zeal, and say they would have served the Christian community better by going into hiding, thus conserving their strength for the service of the Church. But in the light of faith, we have to admit that the martyr's complete sacrifice and total self-gift to God surpasses every other practice of Christian charity. It is also worth adding that the hermit, like the martyr, also exercises charity towards the neighbour, and on a higher level. There are different ways of exercising charity: just like those directed to corporal needs, works of charity to meet spiritual needs have their place. In his life of prayer, the hermit does not cut himself off from the community; like the martyr, he becomes an intercessor for his fellows, in a holocaust which also bears fruit for the Christian community. This is a form of neighbourly charity which is very necessary and remarkably effective.

Further, and beyond all that, monastic history shows that in times of persecution and great calamities the hermits did not self-centredly shut themselves up in their seclusion, leaving the Christians dwelling in the world to bear the weight of the struggle. Always they gave up their beloved solitude in order to help their brothers and suffer with them. So it is clear that the hermit, too, fulfils the fundamental Christian commandment, and that in a very perfect way. Nor should we forget the exercise of the charity which, among hermits, unites the spiritual father and his son; we shall have occasion to say more of this relationship.

There is also the fact that Jesus himself and his Apostles did not lead a hermit life, but rather a sort of community life, they never completely withdrew from the world, except for a very limited spell of time. But this cannot be seriously taken as an objection against the hermit life. Indeed, the ways in which Christian life has been lived and the differing charisms are not always the same in the Church, or at any rate have not always had the same external expression. So it was that the hermit life was born in the Church during an era following Christianity's beginnings; the Apostolic period was over, and martyrdom had become very rare. Even so, nothing prevents us from adopting the view of St Nilus and other Fathers, who saw the eremitical life as the continuation of the life of renunciation in the Apostolic age. As will be seen later, monastic life, particularly in its eremitic form, has very close links with martyrdom, of which we can see it as the continuation. The Church always needs martyrs, because the Church of Jesus Christ is essentially the Church of martyrs. In times of peace, when the storm of persecution is past, the Church still has her martyrs; these do not soak the sand of the arenas with their blood, but rather, without shedding their blood, draw down on the world an abundant outpouring of divine grace through their prayers and mortifications. These are the monks and hermits.

* * *

St Thomas is echoed, with no less authority, by Pius XI, who proclaimed that the Latin Church has never ceased to affirm the primacy of the eremitical life. In an Apostolic Constitution

The Hermit Life

of 15th October 1924[15], the Pope spoke about the Carthusian life. He said, "One could not imagine a more perfect form of life to offer people than that which, with the help of divine grace, is embraced by the Carthusians." He compared the hermits to Moses praying on the mountain; these are victims and holocausts offered to God for their own salvation and for their neighbour's. The Pope went on with broad strokes to summarize the history of the monastic order. He spoke of the ancient ascetics who lived within the bosom of the Church community and went on from there to explain the origins of the anchorites and the cenobitic life. Eremitism was a great gift to the Church, even though the monks bound themselves to abstain from all external ministry to devote themselves entirely to contemplation.

> Which very institution, completely self-contained, so that the monks, each enclosed in his own cell, free from all external ministry and involvement, might devote their souls to heavenly things alone, was of so great and such wonderful advantage to Christian society.[16]

With the passage of time, the primitive fervour cooled, even among the hermits; and with the slackening of discipline, largely due to responsibilities more appropriate to Institutes of active life, it was not long before an almost complete decadence set in. The Church, however, maintained her concern, desiring to see such an important institution flourish again. The hermit life, Pius XI went on, is especially necessary in our own days, when the supernatural is always pushed into the background, when it is not totally ignored.

It might be argued that such a way of life does not suit twentieth century dynamism, that now is the time for apostles and men of action. In the papal document we find once more, in clear and precise terms, the reply which has always been given to such objections: that it is not those who devote themselves to the care of souls who are most useful to the Church, but those whose task is constantly to pray and mortify themselves.

---

15 *Acta Apostolicae Sedis*, 1924, p. 385, Annus XVI, Vol. XVI, 15 Octobris 1924, Num. 10.
16 Pius XI, Apostolic Constitution *Umbratilem* (trans.)

It may easily be understood that those who assiduously fulfil their ministry of prayer and penance do much more for the growth of the Church and the salvation of the human race than those who serve by labouring in the Lord's field.[17]

Pius XI, then, supports the traditional thesis of the necessity of the purely contemplative life, such as is practised by hermits. Hermits are absolutely necessary to the Church, and when the Church thought there was danger of its collapse, she intervened to give new life, through appropriate reforms, to the institution which had fed its life and growth through so many centuries.

* * *

We said earlier that the ancient eremitical ideal had been more authentically preserved in the Eastern Church. "The eremitical life, as it was known in the first centuries of monastic history," writes Friedrich Heiler in his recent work, "has never been lacking in the Eastern Church.... The later organisations of monastic life have always left plenty of scope to the desert life. So it is that eremitical life has retained its primacy over cenobitical life."[18] St Basil the Great reformed monasticism by giving it a definitive cenobitic cast. In his view, the social life of the primitive Christian communities was to be seen, not merely as the model for the life of the simple faithful, but also for the ascetic, hence his insistence on the necessity of fraternal charity. As far as he was concerned, neither the life of the primitive Church nor the exercise of charity received sufficient allowance in the hermit's existence. Furthermore, it did not offer the gifts it had received from the Lord to the service of the community. Finally, to emphasize further his case for the common life, St Basil appealed to St Paul's teaching on the mystical body of Jesus Christ

It is a remarkable fact that, despite the insistence of a saint of such authority and the weighty reasons put forward in favour of cenobitic life, the Eastern Church has always held that the eremitic ideal was incontestably superior. An interesting

---

17 *Ibid.*
18 Friedrich Heiler, *Urkirche und Ostkirche*, 1937, p. 367

The Hermit Life

confirmation of this can be found in the theory of Simeon of Thessalonica (+1428), according to whom Jesus Christ himself is both the source and model of the eremitical life; the example for the cenobites, in contrast, is the life of the Apostles.[19]

The preference of each Church for one or the other form of ascesis can only be explained, as we said earlier, as the consequence of different mentalities, which approach theological problems from different viewpoints. If, as Simeon of Thessalonica says, Jesus Christ himself is the ideal of the hermit monk, that comes down to saying that the monk's goal is "divinization", perfect assimilation to the Man-God, to Christ. "Divinization" as the final perfection of mankind is one of the fundamental theses of the Greek Church. Obviously, this becoming God, sharing in the divine nature, is not to be understood in a pantheist sense; it means a sharing attainable by the creature through sanctifying grace, an idea that is truly central to Greek theology. The influence of neo-Platonic philosophy on Oriental theology's concept of God is undeniable, particularly in the areas of God's simplicity and unity. God's absolute transcendence, and especially the fact that God is above things that multiply, diversify and change, makes God the prime Being, an absolutely simple reality, one and immutable. Man who, by the gift of grace and continuous ascetic effort, is to reach likeness to God, necessarily tends towards being an image of God's simplicity and unity, and this by mortification of his passions which made him a divided and changeable being. The closer he comes to "deification", the closer he comes to the perfect simplicity of God, who is self-sufficient, seeking nothing outside himself. It is clear that a theology which gives such importance to the concept of "deification", and which primarily conceives God as one being, simple and sufficient unto himself, will be led to think of the ideal of Christian perfection in terms of a man completely free of passions and drawn by as perfect an imitation as possible to unity and simplicity, and this indeed is the ideal of the hermit monk.

---

19 Simeon of Thessalonica, PG 155, 913A–C, *Responsa ad Gabrielem Pentapolitanum*. Quaestio LX, Ecquis primus tradiderit divinum sanctumque habitum monachorum, quare angelicus dicitur, et quae sit illius traditi ratio.

The theology of the Western Church is, in contrast, more interesting in matters moral. We have only to think of the questions about grace raised by Pelagius, questions quite unknown to Greek theology, at least from that viewpoint. Hence it is not really surprising to find such tendencies in the idea of monastic life itself. It is seen more as exercising the virtues in order to achieve moral perfection, which obviously requires community life, which of itself offers so many opportunities for the practice of virtue. Perhaps that is one of the theological reasons for the Western Church's preference for cenobitic life.

These different points of view, characteristic of the two Churches, do not exclude one another, it would be more correct to say that they are differences of emphasis.

The Eastern Church's concept certainly does not exclude practice of the virtues, rather it presupposes it. The Latin Church's view is not unaware of the ideas of assimilation and the teaching about the primacy of eremitic life in Christian ascesis. Rather these are the theological leanings of the two Churches, which explain in each the predominance of one form of monastic life or the other, even though both are fully agreed, and always have been, on the doctrinal principles of the ascetic and monastic life, and both recognize the superiority of the eremitic life.

Let us sum up. Among the forms of ascetic life, which essentially consists of separation from the world (*extra mundum fieri*), the hermit life must be admitted to be, of itself, the most perfect. This form of life is only the logical consequence of the Christian concept of perfection and the means necessary to attain it. This does not mean that every ascetic has to be a hermit, nor does it mean that no one other than a hermit can attain perfection. It is divine grace which calls those who are to serve God in such an elevated state of life, and no one has the right to embrace such a rare way of life unless called.

CHAPTER 2

Other Forms of the Ascetic Life

WHAT WE SAID ABOUT ASCETIC LIFE in its most perfect form explains its rarity, and that is precisely the perfection which St Thomas demands of the ascetic preparing to confront the desert solitude. The essence of the eremitical life consists of the total renunciation of earthly goods, meaning not merely all right to exercise ownership, but also of all social relationships, even the most basic, and consequently renunciation of all activity within society, whether civil of ecclesiastical. That is such a harsh and demanding sacrifice for human nature that it automatically excludes any idea of a general vocation to that state. It would also be an exaggeration to think that hermit life is the only avenue for Christian ascesis.

We have already mentioned another of these forms, cenobitic life, monastic life lived in common by groups of individuals, whether few or many. Guided by a rule and a superior, they devote themselves to the same exercises of piety and penance, and in the community itself, find the primary means for the development and strengthening of their interior life.

We will study this other way of ascesis more closely and highlight its importance, so as to draw from it the conclusions which seem to us most useful for ascetic life in general.

The absolute separation from the world to which the hermit aspires meets its first hurdle in the material needs of life, from which not even the perfect life is exempt. So, the desire to be a hermit immediately raises two economic questions: how are the solitaries' needs, however reduced they may be, to be met? And how is an outlet to be found for the products of their manual work? Jesus' saying, "If you would be perfect, go, sell what you possess and give to the poor" (Mt. 19:21), was followed to the letter by the hermits. Following the example of the Apostles, they sought to meet their bodily needs and come to the aid of their needy brothers through the work of their hands. Achieving this and simultaneously closing the door to all contact with society was impossible for the single, isolated hermit. From the very beginning, the economic factor was one of the reasons for which hermit life in complete isolation remained very unusual, simply because it was, in practice, almost impossible to live out. There were always regular meetings of the hermits, required by their prayer, which was often in common, and for ascetic teaching. The same economic factors led to a degree of mutual interchange, the purchase of raw material, the distribution and carrying out of work, training in the various crafts, all conspired to break down the walls of isolation, and so, bit by bit, the hermit became a cenobite.

It would be a serious mistake to try to find the origin of cenobitic life purely in a need to meet these material and economic needs, or, worse still, to compare a monastery to an industrial enterprise run on communist principles. Much deeper spiritual reasons are behind cenobitism and the "autarchy" which was to some extent necessary for the avoidance of over-frequent contacts with the world. The conviction that the anchorite's life, the most perfect form of Christian asceticism, was exceptional, requiring a quite special grace, a charism reserved to the chosen few, was the main reason which led, after the first exuberant era of eremitic life, to the foundation of centres of cenobitic life. Martyrdom is not for all; it is a rare occurrence, and so, in monastic circles, the anchorite was soon compared to a martyr. Further, the experience of many hermits showed the Christian people that, besides a special vocation, withdrawal into the desert required careful and detailed preparation, in order to avoid the dangers of a *tabula rasa*, a complete absence of spiritual formation. As we saw, St Thomas put forward the need for exercise in the virtues and formation in matters of the spirit as reasons for the cenobitic life in preparation for the hermit life. From this point of view, the monastery is a school in which one is trained in the desert struggle. This is what Cassian means when he expresses the desire to reach the higher, eremitical degree, after having been schooled among the cenobites.[1] St Benedict echoes Cassian in his Rule. He greatly respects hermits, having experienced for himself the difficult demands of

---

[1] Cassian, Conferences, 18, 16: *John Cassian: The Conferences*. Translated and annotated by Boniface Ramsey, O. P. (Paulist Press, NY 1996; ACW no. 57).

their life, and similarly come to the conclusion that it was not something to be embraced with a novice's enthusiasm, but only after long and serious trial in cenobitic life, because, he says, you need to be fully armed if you are going to defy the human passions in this way and dare to confront the evil one face to face.[2]

It was also perfectly natural to make the sphere of Christian asceticism accessible to all those who, without having the courage or the grace necessary for life in the desert, nonetheless sought to follow Christ in silence and withdrawal. Hermit life demanded a level of asceticism much more severe than that commonly practised in the world. Hence the need for a form of life for those who wished to withdraw from the world, but did not feel called to the desert.

Then there is the fact that the Lord gives some the gifts which flourish best within the bosom of a community. The reciprocal relationships between a community and its members are in this way many and mutually beneficial.

It would therefore be wrong to look on cenobitic life as a relaxed or decadent form of eremitic life. The monastery is primarily a training-ground for those who are called to single combat in the desert; but it also offers, for those not blessed with such a vocation, the best environment for a healthy ascesis.

We should go further: ascetic life practised in common has its own value and function. *It expresses the social character of the Church*, it offers more frequent opportunities to exercise the Christian virtues, charity in particular. In this way we could say that it is the "normal" form of ascetic life lived outside the world, while hermit life, which requires a special charism, is the exception, the rarity.

No one would dream of claiming that every ascetic should become a hermit, but for all that, it does not detract from the fact that the hermit life remains the highest ideal and the supreme norm, the standard of reference against which all the duties of Christian ascesis are measured and given proportion. We could, therefore, look upon the monastery as an extension of the desert on which it is modelled. The love of solitude in

---

2 RB 1:3–4

the cell, for example, is a theme which finds a thousand exponents among the Fathers in their writings, and which is no less a favourite of cenobitic authors. These are just as given to seeing the cell as a safe refuge in which freely to devote themselves to prayer and contemplation.

The idea that perfection could be attained in a monastery was certainly not unknown to the ancient hermits. The *Apophthegms* tell that one day a monk came to consult Abba Joseph, and said to him, "I would like to abandon the monastery and withdraw into solitude." The Abbot replied, "You should remain where your soul finds rest and experiences no hurt." The monk, having admitted that he enjoyed just as much rest in his monastery as in solitude, went on, "Then what advice do you give me?" Far from simply exhorting him to go off into solitude, the Abbot replied, "If you find as much rest in the monastery as in the desert, put your thoughts on the scales, and if you find one or other of them tips the balance, that is the one to follow."

In another place in the *Apophthegms* we read that a hermit who had spent forty years in the desert and the abbot of a great monastery were talking together. The hermit remarked, "During the whole time I have lived in the desert, the sun has never seen me eating." "As for me," replied the Abbot, "the sun has never seen me angry."

* * *

Because the monastery is a "school", a preparation for the hermit life, and because it is modelled on that ascetic ideal, it must, like it, be essentially contemplative, all the more so if, like the first doctors of the Church, one sees the eremitic life as a continuation of the apostolic life.

The apostolic life, like the monastic life, as we shall see, is based on this saying of Jesus: "Come, follow me", the sum of all the evangelical counsels. They are put into practice by a life of complete detachment, directed almost completely towards contemplation. And even if we think about what we said about the primacy of the hermit life in the last chapter, this will be the best way of doing it, because it best realizes the model. Let us suppose for a moment that cenobitical, rather than eremitical,

Other Forms of the Ascetic Life

life was the most perfect form of ascetic life: were that the case, the evangelical counsels would be subordinate to the exterior exercise of charity, which is the most representative and characteristic virtue of the common life. Such an exercise of charity would then constitute the highest ideal of the ascetic life, and the norm and measure of all ascesis; and among the various forms of cenobitic life, the hierarchical primacy would, furthermore, belong, as is clearly expressed among the religious orders of the Catholic Church, to the form of life, to the order, which entirely subordinated the evangelical counsels to the practice of charity, and especially to the apostolate, the noblest exercise of that virtue.

Quite recently it has been affirmed that the great mediaeval religious Orders, the Franciscans and the Dominicans, as well as modern ones like the Jesuits, have given the most authentic interpretation of the evangelical counsels, closest to the original, and in line with the intentions of Christ himself. The same source maintained that the ancient, more contemplative Orders had subordinated the evangelical counsels to personal sanctification, in a sort of "holy egotism". Christ however had ordered the Apostles to proclaim the Gospel throughout the world, rather than commanding them to withdraw into the desert. Above all, in this way he was making clear his desire to help the exercise of the apostolate and Christian charity in all that related to its sphere. The limits set to the contemplative life in modern orders and their clearly apostolic goal, to which the practice of the evangelical counsels is subordinated, has restored the apostolate to the place which it had in the life of Jesus and his Apostles, a place which it henceforth should have in the life of every ascetic and of every true disciple of the Lord.[3]

Clearly, this viewpoint differs from ours; it is incompatible with viewing the hermit life as the form of ascetic life which most authentically realizes the practice of the evangelical counsels. According to this view, cenobitic life should be primarily directed towards action, so that contemplation would be subordinated to active aims. If, on the contrary, one thinks that cenobitic life should find its reference, norm and measure of

---

3 D. Thalhammer S. J., *Jenseitige Menschen. Eine Sinndeutung des Ordensstandes* (Innsbruck 1937), p. 5ff

comparison in eremitical life, then work and exterior activity ought to be subordinated to the claims of contemplation, only forming part of the cenobites' life to the extent that the needs of the community and its members require it.

* * *

We should not confuse the ascetic life of cenobites with the common life of clerks regular and religious belonging to orders with an essentially practical goal. Ascetical and devotional exercises are laid down for them, and a shorter or longer time is set aside for retreat and contemplation, but all that is closely related and subordinated to the precise end which these religious serve. You could in some ways compare their kind of life to that of the first ascetics living in the world, who, while setting aside a time for contemplation, devoted themselves to the service of the faithful and the Church. What distinguishes cenobites from clerks regular is, properly speaking, the problem of work. This is a problem which arises quite differently in each of these cases, and in the light of the different solutions suggested, one can on the one hand clarify the nature of the cenobitic life, and on the other, the ideal sought by clerks regular and modern religious orders.

As we have seen, cenobites are ascetics who do not lead an eremitical life, either because they are still preparing themselves for it, or because they have not received the necessary charism. The hermit is certainly obliged to work, and in any case, contemplation cannot completely dispense him from it, since it is a divine commandment. Further, human nature needs an occupation to give it a break from time to time from the demands of contemplation, to give it a chance to build itself up again in order to raise itself once more towards God with renewed energy. The hermit, all the same, does not organize his work in view of the sole consideration, important though it may be, of his daily bread; he is also drawn to it by his desire for mortification and spiritual growth. This is what leads him to undertake tasks at which the world may smile, but which, despite their simplicity, have a very serious end in view. No more is the cenobite dispensed from the law of work, even less so, since an entire community depends for its subsistence on the work of his hands. Further, again differently

Other Forms of the Ascetic Life

from the hermits, contemplation leaves him greater free time, which he can usefully employ doing his work. It is of the greatest importance to have a proper understanding of the ends of monastic life in choosing work for cenobites. Hence, from what has already been said, one can see why the masters of monastic life prefer manual to intellectual labour, a preference which can be seen in all the great reformers of the monastic Order, all of whom have as their goal something rather more than a simple return to the letter of the Rule of St Benedict. It is easy to state the real reason for this: it is because manual work, rather than being a distraction from contemplation, is rather a help to it, insofar as it represents a penitential activity.

In some situations, intellectual work may be legitimately considered as a prolongation and natural consequence of contemplation, and then it fulfils the role of manual work, if only in part. It acquired the preponderant place which it now has in cenobitic life during the era when monks were raised to the priestly dignity. Under the pressure of urgent need, the Church herself sought the help of the monks, and no-one can deny its right to entrust the care of souls to its ascetics. Again, the cenobite does not live a life as radically separate from society as the hermit; he is merely following the example of the ancient ascetics by working for the Church, and the Church may thus have recourse to him in her need.

The immediate reason for this frankly truly sensational innovation was to be found in the lack of capable priests. From their very beginnings, monasteries had had priest-monks, but they were almost exclusively reserved for the internal needs of the monastery itself, as is still the case in the eastern Church. Ministry outside the cloister, apart from what fell within the limits of "spiritual fatherhood" (of which we will say more later), was unknown. Cassian describes this ancient custom in energetic language and shows us the profound reasons which explain it. In his opinion, and according to the most ancient customs of the Fathers, women and bishops are the two classes of people monks must avoid at all costs.[4]

---

4 Cassian, *Institutes* Book XI, ch. 18, on vainglory: *John Cassian: The*

The hands laid on the monk's head at the moment of ordination burdened him with a set of obligations which were at that time believed to be incompatible with monastic life, for the care of souls demands constant contact with the world, with those persons and things which the monk has abandoned.

Even so, as we have remarked, this burden was imposed by the Church herself, and this custom has been maintained in the West for centuries. Any sensible judge will accept the assent and witness of the centuries to the fact that this development clearly represents a proper adaptation of the monastic ideal to the needs of our Church and to the character of the Western peoples, rather than a distortion. The essentially contemplative goal of monastic life is not diminished thereby. Everything must be subordinated to the essential; even priestly tasks should not be allowed to be an excuse for dilution of the ideal, but should remain in their place in the hierarchy of values. As much as he can, the monk-priest will fulfil his duties within his own monastery, and so demonstrate that *cella continuata dulcescit*, "how delightful it is to dwell continually in one's cell", is a real consolation for him. Relations with seculars should be limited to the indispensable, and works should be chosen which are best suited to foster a regular and recollected life. These should not absorb so much time and energy that they leave no more than the necessary minimum time for the duties of the contemplative life. The clerk regular's life is organized quite differently, his priestly duties come first and receive all the space they need, and his devotions and ascetic activities are made to fit in with these.

Different attitudes to work, diverse but not opposed, can be seen in the lives of monks and regular clerics. The regular cleric does not primarily devote himself to contemplation, but to activity, in the exercise of his priestly duties. From the very fact of his vocation, he does not live separated from the world, except to the extent that every zealous priest and disciple of Jesus Christ should so do; rather, he lives and moves within the world, in order to fulfil his apostolic mission; his holiness comes through the practice of a most exalted ministry, and he

---

Conferences. Translated and annotated by Boniface Ramsey, O. P., Paulist Press, NY 1996 (ACW no. 57).

sacrifices himself for the good of souls.

A clear understanding of these matters is indispensable, especially for candidates to the monastic life, otherwise one risks having, sooner or later, sad surprises.

* * *

The theory of ascetic life which we have been portraying may seem too "monastic", in the sense of making it seem that every ascetic ought to conform to the cenobitic ideal. Since there are not two ideals of perfection — the monk and the Christian living in the world aspire to the same perfection — it will be obvious that monastic life and ascetic life outside the monastery must be related; it is simply that the monk makes use of means which allow him greater freedom in that quest. Of itself, monastic life is no guarantee of attaining holiness, and does not produce a perfection distinct from that sought by the "ordinary" Christian. St John Chrysostom has very clearly pointed out the identity of the two ideals, "Those who live in the world, although they are married, should be just like monks in everything else."[5]

The desert ascetics were well aware that complete separation from the world, together with the most austere works of penance, were not enough. Abba Antony, living in solitude, one day learned in a vision that a man of holiness equal to his own was working as a physician in the world; he had given to the poor everything superfluous to his needs, and all day long he sang the Trisagion (the "*Holy, holy, holy*") in union with the angelic choir.[6] The great holiness and extraordinary asceticism of Christians living in the world was also revealed to other solitaries.

St John Chrysostom particularly reminded married couples that it was possible for them to lead an ascetic life, and described its chief characteristics. The ideal of perfection is the same, monks and lay-people seek the same goal. The means they use are the same: mortification, prayer, reading sacred texts. Such

---

5   John Chrysostom, *Homilies on the Letter to the Hebrews* 7, 41: Opera Omnia, T. XII, Cap. IV, Hom VII, col. 113B, ed. Bernardi de Montfaucon OSB (Mauriust edition), Ed. Parisina altera, emendata et aucta, Paris 1838.
6   Abba Antony, PG 65, 84C, *Apophthegmata Patrum*, Appendix ad Palladium, Antony 24

is, at base, the teaching of St John Chrysostom. It is quite clear that he was not trying to revolutionize the world by turning it into one great monastery, but equally clear that he viewed monastic life as a model for every Christian. As Pourrat remarks, "People did not, during the Patristic era, write spiritual works for the faithful living in the world.... There were not two distinct spiritualities.... There was only one: monastic spirituality."[7]

St John Chrysostom was not of course unaware of the usual objections raised against such a view:

> I must devote myself to public affairs, I am a craftsman, I am married, I must concern myself with the education of my children, look after my family; I am a man of the world, I don't have the time to read the Scriptures, I have to leave all that to those who have abandoned the world in order to withdraw to the tops of the highest mountains and live in complete retreat.[8]

But the saint will not accept these excuses; marriage itself is no obstacle to perfection. The commandments have the same force for everybody. When the Lord gives a piece of advice not intended to oblige everybody, he makes it quite clear:

> If marriage or the education of children were to be an obstacle to the way of virtue, then the Creator of the world would not have instituted them, were they to be in the way of such an important and essential goal. Marriage is not an obstacle, when lived chastely, in accordance with the commandments of the divine law. It even brings great consolations, it destroys nature's unhealthy impulses and prevents natural energies from raging like the waves of a storm-tossed sea, and brings the vessel safely to harbour.[9]

---

7 Pierre Pourrat, *La spiritualité chrétienne*, I, IX
8 John Chrysostom, *Hom. de Lazaro* 3, I; John Chrysostom, Four discourses, chiefly on the parable of the Rich man and Lazarus (1869) Discourse 3. pp. 59–89. Early Church Fathers—Additional Texts.
9 John Chrysostom, *In Gen.* 21, 12: *St. John Chrysostom, Homilies on Genesis, 18–45*, Translated by Robert C. Hill, FOTC Vol. 89 (CUA Press, 1990), p. 59.

Other Forms of the Ascetic Life

In St John Chrysostom's writings, (by which he seeks to instruct in the true ascesis which all, whether monks or not, must practise), the most-frequently occurring points are prayer, charity, restrained use of this world's goods, regular reading of Holy Scripture.

In the matter of prayer, the saint makes demands that would be astonishing nowadays. He asks, for example, that in the very middle of the night, all, father, mother and children, should arise to praise God,

> The night is not made just for sleep and rest.... Arise, gaze on the choir of the stars. What deep silence, what great peace! The soul then feels clearer, lighter, more ethereal, as though set free by the sublime. The silent majesty of the darkness invites us to compunction. Get down on your knees; pray; ask God to be merciful. Nocturnal prayer moves him more. You, man, should act like this, not just leave it to your wife. The house ought continually to be an oratory for husband and wife.... If you have sons and daughters, wake them up, and then your house will be like a church during the night; if you have young children, who need more sleep, let them recite some short prayers, and then go back to sleep.[10]

The ideal advocated by St John Chrysostom is certainly very demanding, and yet a situation described in so much detail seems unlikely to be something entirely made up. Further, there are, perhaps, still many today who without knowing it, still follow the teachings of such a demanding Father.

Having sketched out the most common forms of ascetic life and having come to the conclusion that they all reflect the same ideal, we should now study an aspect common to every form of ascesis, and which in faithfulness to the whole of Christian tradition, we will describe as *Deum quaerere*, to seek God.

---

10 John Chrysostom, *Hom. In Act.* 26, 3, following; *The Homilies of S. John Chrysostom on the Acts of the Apostles*, translated with notes and indices. Part I. *Hom. I–XXVIII*. (Oxford John Henry Parker, F & J Rivington, London, 1851), p. 378.

The ascetic "seeks" God; he wishes to free himself from all that he knows of the world, in order to clear the paths of that quest, which despite all efforts, is still choked with a thousand obstacles. The word *quaerere*, to seek, expresses both the ardour of the desire and the difficulty of the task, rather than *accedere*, to attain to, which besides the joy that this meeting would give us, would seem to suggest that it would require of us a scarcely significant effort. It is only after death, when we have finally broken every earthly resistance, that we will be able to *accedere*, go to meet the Lord; at present we are limited to *quaerere*, to "seeking" him.

From the merely intellectual point of view, we could speak of "approaching" God, even with both feet still firmly on the ground. From the seriousness of their work, the profundity of their scientific research and the study of the most difficult problems, the philosopher and the scientist approach God intellectually. Clearly, this is an imperfect route, difficult and demanding, not open to all, but to those who follow it faithfully, it guarantees progress, admittedly slow, but progressive, even if limited to the spheres of science and nature. That is not so in the case of the Christian ascetic. In his journey towards God, he does not find the road broad and trouble-free; his task goes beyond the clear methods built on reason and used by the scientist. The ascetic is compelled to admit the powerlessness of his nature to achieve a goal as demanding as the attainment of his personal perfection. He does not rely on his will alone to progress and reach his end, or even simply for a beginning, and that is why his task really does involve "seeking God".

Anyone who always follows the same course and is hidebound in method is not seeking God—that is not to say that instability is what characterizes the ascetic, but rather that freedom of spirit demands a certain flexibility in the matter of spiritual practices, and thus the ascetic alternates times of prayer and peaceful meditation, penitential exercises, the practice of the virtues, study and prayer. In all these, he seeks God, and does not worry himself about when or how God will come and visit him. God is the one who chooses the moment of encounter with the soul, not the ascetic. We cannot force a meeting on the Lord, our part is to stay awake, keep an ear open as it were, so as to recognize his voice among the noises which the disordered world might muffle. That is how to "seek God".

But "seeking God" means more than this. Christian asceticism is categorically opposed to quietism — so from this point of view, the ascetic's dynamism ought to appeal to our age. His quest is unwearying, and only ceases with death. If someone is searching, it implies that he has lost something. The ascetic seeks God, because he is convinced that he has lost him, and this awful loss was caused by our first parents' sin. If we want to rediscover God, we must go back on our tracks. This thought was dear to St Benedict, who passed it on to his disciples: in the Prologue to his Rule he tells the postulant to take up the weapons of obedience, so that by using them he may return to him from whom the idleness of disobedience had separated him. Gregory illustrates the same thought, when he tells what St Benedict's sons saw at the moment of his death: from the saint's cell up to highest heaven a path was marked out, strewn with rich cloths and shining with innumerable lights.

* * *

Paradise, the delightful home of our first parent, is still our homeland too, even if it was lost by sin. It is the secondary goal of the ascetic's quest, after God. By returning to Paradise and to his Lord, he will recover all the rights that were part of his citizenship as he had them before. This world below is, as far as he is concerned, a place of exile. His native place can only be his true and real native land, the land which exceeds every desire, where ineffable joy and peace reign. Were this not so, then Paradise would be no more than a brilliant metaphor, rather than being the country of the elect which it is. But because it is indeed a reality, the ascetic leaves everything, even his country, in order to possess it. The saying, *extra mundum factus*, set apart from the world, applies to every ascetic, not merely to the monk, (because there is no asceticism without some sort of separation from the world), and this shows how completely true it is. During his mortal life, the ascetic is nothing but a traveller, he is ceaselessly journeying towards the object of his desires, he is always on the way. That is why the word *synodia* is often applied to groups of ascetics, because it means "caravan" — a group of travellers who have left the world and are on their way back to their true homeland, paradise.

Obviously one cannot speak of *stabilitas loci*, stability of place, in these terms, it has a special meaning. Strictly speaking, the monk's or the ascetic's stability does not mean that they have found their real home in the country or the place where they are living. If an ascetic took no account of such a basic concept, but attached himself to a single spot on this earth, it would imply that he had lost sight of the ideal behind his vocation, and indeed that his vocation was imperilled. From time to time, God also uses providential means, such as persecution, expulsion and confiscation, to remind us that we are still far from home, and so keeps us on track.

Even though, even humanly speaking, the ascetic is a real blessing for the place where he abides, that is not to be seen as one of his essential roles; yes, there is a social function to fulfil, but that is not what really concerns him. His place of residence is not his true homeland; just as he no longer belongs to the world, so his native land, the place where he passes his life and the place of his burial, are equally foreign to him. He is *extra mundum*, outside the world, and consequently *extra patriam*, outside his native land.

The geographical siting of many monasteries tends to confirm this fact. Institutes and orders with a more active bent pitch their tents in centres of population—capital cities, towns, urban centres where their sorts of works can be more easily developed, whereas monks, on the contrary, populate solitary valleys, steep rocks, the mountain peaks, just as Monte Cassino in Italy or Montserrat in Spain have done. The reason for the founders of these monasteries choosing these places was not some sort of romantic fantasy, they had a quite different motive: far from towns, from their own country, from their parents, monks ought to be separated from the world, and the monastery's site ought in some sense to bring this about, or at any rate constantly remind the monks of their separation.

* * *

Other Forms of the Ascetic Life

The search for God and the quest for a lost paradise is, at least in part, at the root of that very specialized form of asceticism practised by gyrovague monks. Influenced by the ideas we have been propounding, these ascetics abandoned their own countries in order to wander about, never establishing their dwelling in any one place. They were the first monastic nomads. This was admittedly a quite unique and original form of asceticism, a concrete expression of the search for God and quest for Paradise. Clearly, such a lifestyle had many disadvantages and could lend itself to all sorts of abuses. Spiritual intentions were soon snuffed out by material considerations, leading headlong to decadence and disaster, so that by St Benedict's day the depraved life of the gyrovagues had become a scandal, leading him, despite his habitual restraint, to condemn them unreservedly and rate them as the lowest form of monastic life. Still, even in our own days, it is not difficult to find ascetics who have practised this unusual form of asceticism. It is enough to mention St Benedict Joseph Labre, who died in 1793, after spending his whole life as a beggar and pilgrim, destitute of everything and seeking only God. The fact that he has been canonized shows that this form of asceticism is formally recognized by the Church and is not just a human fancy. In this way the Church assures us that the saint who constantly wandered the face of the earth, ardently desiring that Heaven for which he unremittingly strove, finally reached his true homeland and there found the eternal rest that every Christian thirsts for, whatever external form of ascetic life he adopts.

CHAPTER 3

Imitation of Christ

THE ASCETIC LIFE IS A PILGRIMAGE, A journey which ends in Paradise. The ascetic seeks God, is in search of that original homeland lost by sin. Every ascetic's life in some way reflects this truth, although it is most clearly seen in the hermit's life, devoting his whole being to the search for God, he abandons everything, even externals such as homeland and family, that might be an obstacle to his quest for God.

Even so, if you had asked one of the ancient ascetics or one of the first hermits, why he was so completely separating himself from the world, it is not likely that he would have replied that it was so that he could rediscover Paradise or do battle with the devil; more probably he would have replied, in order to follow Jesus Christ and imitate him.

In the most ancient witnesses, the real reason for conversion to ascetic or monastic life is frequently given as imitation of Christ. We know how important the Gospel call was in the life of St Antony, "If you would be perfect, go, sell what you possess, and give to the poor, and you will have treasure in heaven; then come, follow me" (Mt. 19:21). These words led him to distribute his goods to the poor and withdraw into the desert. St Pachomius demanded that candidates for monastic life renounce the world and their own wills, and persevere in imitating Our Lord who taught us to do so. That is what, so he says, is meant by "taking up your cross."[1] St Benedict describes the new monk as a soldier of Jesus Christ who follows his leader in taking up the arms of obedience.[2] Further on he speaks of obedience in the following terms, "There is no doubt that whoever does this is fulfilling that word of the Lord, who said, 'I have not come to do my own will, but that of him who sent me'."[3] Another

---

1 Vita, 16, AA. SS., Mai III, 301 (Pachomius)Vita S. Pachomii Abbatis, die decima quarta Maii, §16, p. 301.
2 RB, Prol. 3
3 RB 5:13

monastic document of the same era puts it thus, "Down there I saw many Fathers leading an angelic life, advancing in the imitation of our Lord Jesus Christ."[4]

It is quite clear that the ultimate reason for monastic life is imitation of Christ, just as it is the bedrock of any truly Christian life. Imitation of Christ is the reason for every aspect of ascesis: detachment from the world, because Jesus rejected this world's values; battle with the devil, since Jesus came down from heaven to destroy Satan's realm; return to Paradise, the paradise he promised on Golgotha, "Today you will be with me in Paradise" (Lk. 23:43).

By going more deeply into the imitation of Christ, we will discover the very heart of Christian asceticism.

* * *

"Imitation of Christ" means two things: first, that we are supposed to model our lives on Christ, and second, that we are to follow Jesus, who has led the way by himself following the way which leads back to the Father. These two aspects of imitation of Christ are inseparable, though the second enjoys a certain relatively greater importance, because when we follow Christ's way and carry our cross after him, we are modelling our lives on his and shaping our souls to his divine example.

If we are to follow Christ's footsteps, we need to know the way by which he went. He tells us what that is, in very few words, "I came from the Father and have come into the world; again, I am leaving the world and am going to the Father" (Jn. 16:28). This descent from the bosom of the Father to the world and departure from the world to return to the Father is in three stages. The first is, "I came from the Father", the act of coming down from heaven to earth, which the Christian ascetic imitates in leaving family and country, to become like him, a pilgrim far from his native land. The first ascetics saw this prefigured in God's command to Abraham, "Leave your country, leave your family." As will be seen, this first step is the best foundation for the exercise of the virtue of humility.

---

4 *Paradisum Patrum*, History of the Monks of Egypt (P. G. 65, 443B)

The second stage is identified with Jesus Christ's life on earth, "I have come into the world." There we find the Passion and Resurrection, that was why Christ dwelt among us, so that he could die and rise, so as to free us from sin. There, too, the ascetic seeks to imitate the Lord — by mortification, by exercising obedience, he shares, if only mystically, in the death and resurrection of Christ, because he did not become incarnate to do his own will, but the will of Him who sent him. The third and last stage of our Lord's course, "I am leaving the world and going to the Father", is seen in his Ascension, which the ascetic imitates in a mystical lifting up of the soul in prayer. Let us concentrate for the time being on the first two stages and how they are reproduced in the ascetic life; we will deal with the third stage when we come to the chapters on the life of prayer.

* * *

"I came from the Father" sums up the first stage, which contains the mystery of the Incarnation, Christ's appearing in the world. It is scarcely credible that the second divine person should leave the bosom of the Father in order to come down to earth: "He came to his own home, and his own people received him not" (Jn. 1:11). Christ truly became a pilgrim. There is no shortage of images which have come down to us from antiquity, illustrating this idea: the divine Word, dressed like a pilgrim, takes leave of the Father, to come into the world and begin his work of Redemption as an unknown stranger. This is the basis of the title, "Pilgrim", sometimes applied to our divine Saviour.

Obviously, this title could be mis-read and understood in heterodox fashion. It might lead someone to think — as has indeed happened — that Jesus Christ possessed nothing of our mortal fleshly nature, that he only looked like a man, without being so in fact, that he came among us as a pilgrim, but in a nature entirely different from ours. We will limit ourselves to pointing out that this implies some sort of dualism, which regards our human flesh as too unworthy, or rather, too radically contaminated with evil, to be capable of really being taken up by the Word of God. The consequence would be that any disciple of Jesus Christ who might want to follow in his steps would have to free himself completely not merely from human nature's needs, but even from human nature itself, leading to a distorted mortification which could only result in destruction.

But that is not the Catholic understanding of the meaning of the title of "Pilgrim", applied to Jesus Christ. He had a true human nature, just like ours, inherited from Adam our first parent. So, in calling him Pilgrim, we don't mean that he is not truly a man, but that he came down from heaven of his own will, that he became poor, unknown, scorned, for our sake he veiled the outward splendour of his glory, even though he is free both from personal sin and from the original sin.

The ascetic who imitates Jesus Christ also becomes a pilgrim, separating himself from all that humanly speaking he holds dear. Like Jesus Christ, who "did not count equality with God a thing to be grasped, but emptied himself" (Phil. 2:6ff), he too has laid aside all his earthly possessions, so as to imitate the voluntary humiliation of the Master. The phrase, *Nudum Christum nudi sequentes*,[5] "nakedly following the naked Christ", expresses a similar thought. Thus, sometimes, the ascetics gave up even their clothes, in order to imitate Christ's complete stripping of his heavenly glory.

This idea found receptive ears, because philosophy had already prepared the ground, espousing the idea of "nakedness" as a divine ideal; Seneca, for instance said "Silver does not make us like God, for God possesses nothing, not even clothing: *Deus nudus est*, God is naked"[6] God needs nothing, the same is true of the monk, since he is trying to make himself like God. St Jerome takes up the same thought, applying it to Christ and to the monk, "If I have enough to feed and clothe myself, I shall be content, for I shall follow the naked cross nakedly."[7] The saint does not here mean a complete absence of clothing, when he speaks of nakedness, but rather detachment from all superfluous and useless goods. Elsewhere he goes back to this

---

5 *Vita Mariani Scotti*, I, I *AA. SS.*, II, Febr., 364
6 *Ep.* 4, 7: Seneca the Younger, Ep. XXXI, Loeb Classical Library, p. 226
7 Jerome, *Ep.*, 52, 5: *Select letters of St. Jerome*, with English translation by F. A. Wright, (Heinemann, London; Harvard University Press, Cambridge MA, 1963), p. 200. Loeb Classical Library. PL. 22, 531, *ad Nepotianum*.

Imitation of Christ

thought, "Naked, I follow the naked cross, and so I will more easily be able to climb Jacob's ladder."[8] It is an idea which is very familiar to ascetic tradition.

Imitation of Christ coming down to earth and his wandering life gave rise to another form of asceticism: ascetic pilgrimages. Ascetics set off for a distant, foreign land, as a tangible, concrete way of putting detachment from family and country into practice. This is *xeniteia* and means those who have left their country out of love for Christ, not at all the same as the blameworthy gyrovague monks, mentioned earlier. As everyone knows, love for one's natal place is a sentiment dear to the human heart. At the same time as he breaks off his family ties, the ascetic must separate himself from any element of his love for his earthly country which might, however slightly, distance him from, or divert him from his love of his heavenly homeland. Clearly, just like love for those who are dear to us, love for country can be a virtue. Here, however, we are talking about a special impulse of grace, leading someone to sacrifice what he holds dearest. It is, after all, logical that anyone who leaves father, mother, brothers and sisters to follow Jesus Christ should not allow themselves to be held back by an all-too-natural love for their country. God is not served in one place alone, and one place is not better than another for serving him. Breaking off our attachments to our earthly homeland is one of the most effective ascetical tools for bringing about a complete detachment from the things of this world and making the ascetic more like Jesus Christ, who abandoned everything for our sakes, and "annihilated himself".

This led Abba Jacob to say, "It is greater to be a guest than to receive a guest."[9]

The subject of *xeniteia* leads on another ascetical practice, *stenochoria*. This means stability in a specific place, quite strictly defined, from which the ascetic may not wander. One who has quit his country out of love for God can quite easily settle

---

8   Jerome, Ep. 58, 2; *The Letters of S. Jerome: A selection*, The Latin text by Rev. James Duff, MA, Browne & Nolan, Dublin, nd, p. 220. PL 22, *ad Paulinum*.

9   *Apophthegmata Patrum*, PG 65, 231C, Appendix ad Palladium, Abba Jacob, n.1.

down in a new abode, so, to avoid setting up new ties, the pilgrim ascetic limits himself to one small corner, avoiding new relationships so as to give himself completely to love of Jesus Christ and desire for the heavenly homeland. When, for whatever reason, *xeniteia* has become impossible, *stenochoria* has often been a replacement for it. *Xeniteia* has not disappeared in our own day, but its real ascetic value is not usually appreciated, and it is usually subordinated to practical needs, as in the case of missionary congregations. It is also very difficult to observe nowadays, given the multiple legal constraints which bind people to their countries. However that may be, the ascetic must in some way or other acquire a certain freedom of spirit; he must watch himself closely so as not to drift into a form of patriotism incompatible with Christian charity, which refuses to make distinctions between people, countries or races. Again, in monasteries there exists the institution known as enclosure, a part (which may be small or large) of the place which is forbidden to outsiders. Monks may not go out from it without the express permission of the superior. It is true that the obligations imposed by priestly ministry often obliges them to leave their enclosure, but more strictly contemplative orders, such as the Trappists, and, of course, the nuns, observance of enclosure is very strict. It imposes a brake on the natural need to move around, thereby involving a continual mortification, and finds its justification in imitation of Christ, who became a pilgrim for us. Enclosure separates the monk from the world and immerses him in a heavenly atmosphere, focuses him on the Godly life.

Both *xeniteia* and *stenochoria* are closely related to another ascetic practice: silence. The masters of the spiritual life are untiring in stating repeatedly how necessary and how advantageous it is. Later on, we will develop considerably the theme of the positive value of silence, which, apart from being a mortification and renunciation of social relationships, is primarily a positive contributor to the interior life. For the moment, it is enough to note that both *xeniteia* and *stenochoria* tend to separate the ascetic from the world, but that this separation is not fully realized except to the extent that the tongue is controlled, because *xeniteia* and *stenochoria* would be fruitless if the were not accompanied by silence. The first monks were well aware of this: "If you cannot control your tongue, you will never be a pilgrim, no matter where you go, *Non eris peregrinus quocumque abieris.*"[10] "True *xeniteia* consists of controlling your own tongue."[11]

Imitation of Christ the pilgrim has inspired many ascetics to go on pilgrimage, and monastic history offers not a few cases of monks who began their ascetic "career" by going on a pilgrimage. That is an easier way to go as a foreigner to another country than *xeniteia*. After his pilgrimage, the monk returns home to his own country to begin a new life. The temporary separation from his country during his pilgrimage will have severed many attachments which formerly bound him to people and things. He returns from his pilgrimage liberated and renewed. Usually, after his return, he lives as hidden away as possible—the story of St Alexis, who after returning from pilgrimage, for the rest of his life lived unrecognized as a beggar outside his father's house, is a good illustration of this.

These pilgrimages had another advantage. The monk would visit other ascetics and enrich himself with their spiritual treasures, and when he returned would pass on the wisdom of these holy old men to his brothers, rather like St Martin, for example. The similar journey made by John Cassian, deserves to be described as religious exploration: he made efforts to come to know all the ascetics and become acquainted with the teachings of each great centre of asceticism.

This reminds us that the ascetic, spiritual life is not an art attainable merely by book-learning, nor by solitary or individual practice. Rather it requires a master who is himself an ascetic, and not a mere professor of ascesis. Later we will see how necessary and beneficial it is to be in contact with a master who is an ascetic not only personally experienced, but more, who has attained a certain degree of perfection in the spiritual life.

So the monk, having had the benefit of the words and example of one or more masters, fathers of spiritual life, returned to his own country, trained in the art of perfection. Becoming

10 *Apophthegmata Patrum*, PG 65, 255D; Alphabetical collection, de abbate Longino 1 (76); Solesmes 449 Longin.
11 *Ibid.*

a pilgrim with Christ and for Christ was something so deeply rooted in the hearts of the ascetics that they liked to call themselves *peregrinus*, "pilgrim", because the word constantly reminded the monk of that principle of the ascetic life, that he was to imitate Jesus Christ, who had become a pilgrim for us, and that he was to desire intensely the heavenly homeland that we have lost.

Imitation of Christ the pilgrim brings us back to that conception of the ascetic life which we described earlier, the idea that the ascetic must separate and distance himself from the world, a separation which the hermit and the "pilgrim" bring about in a special way. Every form of ascesis must in some way or other relate to this principle of imitation of Christ. Every ascetic, whatever the outward form his life may take, far from thinking of this earth as a lasting dwelling, must behave like a foreigner and pilgrim and experience a certain feeling of alienation from his surroundings. Otherwise, he has no right to say he is truly an imitator of Jesus Christ, the first and greatest pilgrim, he cannot claim to be following in his footsteps.

* * *

In a Lenten sermon which traces the idea of detachment from the world, St Bernard used the figure of the pilgrim ascetic as an illustration. His words eloquently confirm what we have just said.

> Happy are those who, in this world of sin, behave like pilgrims and guests and manage to remain unharmed by it. Alas, we have here no stable dwelling, and we sigh for that which will afterwards be ours.... The pilgrim marches on the royal road, without wandering off to left or right. Nothing can worry him or hold him back. He sighs for his true country, he is intent on it; happy if he has food and something to cover him, he does not want to be a burden on anyone.[12]

---

12 Bernard, *Sermo de peregrino mortuo et crucifixo*: Bernard of Clairvaux, *Sermons for Lent and the Easter Season*, trans. Irene Edmonds, reviewed by John Leinenweber, ed. & rev. by Mark A. Scott, OCSO, Introduction by Wim Verbaal, Cistercian Fathers Series No. 52 (Cistercian Publications,

The saint goes on to say that one can also go higher, for even if the pilgrim does not join those who have citizen rights in the world, he still sometimes rejoices over what he sees or hears from others, or what he may tell others he has seen. "Obviously that cannot stop his progress, but it can delay him on his way, leading him briefly to forget his country, less spurred-on by the desire to reach it. Someone who is "dead" is better than he is." One who is dead, even if not yet buried, does indeed not notice anything or feel insult or praise, nothing makes any impression on him. "O happy death which keeps us unstained, because it makes us complete strangers to the world." In that outburst of scorn full of St Paul's most noble sentiments, St Bernard sees a still more sublime death, "Far be it from me to glory except in the cross of our Lord Jesus Christ, by which the world has been crucified to me, and I to the world" (Gal. 6:14). Beyond mere death to the world, the ascetic is crucified to the world.

> All that the world loves is a cross for you: the pleasures of the flesh, honours, riches, men's empty praises. . . . Is this degree not higher than the first and the second? The pilgrim who wishes to live in complete harmony with his calling, scorns everything earthly, even if doing so sometimes breaks his heart. The dead remain unmoved by praise or blame. For him who has been raised to the third heaven, everything that the world loves is a cross, and everything that the world regards as a cross is loved by him.

It was by such thoughts as these that St Bernard exhorted his brethren to ever-greater detachment from the things of this world.

The basic idea of his teaching is in complete agreement with what we have been saying. The ascetic is a pilgrim and must detach himself from the joys of the world. In magisterial terms, St Bernard seeks to lead his monks to ever-greater detachment, with the goal of reaching the same detachment as Jesus the pilgrim, dead and crucified. It is worth noting that St Bernard relates the highest degree of detachment to St Paul's rapture to

---

Liturgical Press, Collegeville, Minnesota, 2013), Sermon 6, 1, p. 49, 'Of the Pilgrim, the Dead and the Crucified'.

the third heaven — this is deliberate, not mere chance, because for St Bernard the highest mystical summits go together with the most perfect detachment, further proof that mysticism and asceticism are inseparable.

* * *

Christ, who became a traveller among men, emptied himself completely. The pilgrim ascetic must follow in his footsteps, and bring about in himself Christ's total self-emptying, and this will be the directing principle of his moral life. There is only one word which sums up all he seeks to achieve: humility.

Trying to justify the ascetic life for any other reason would simply be to go astray. How could anyone claim to have understood the essence of the monastic life, if he persisted in the view that living as a monk meant following the most obvious teachings of reason? That would be to cheapen the sublime beauty of Christian asceticism, which does not find its guiding principles in philosophy's fragile teachings, but rather in the living example of Our Lord. The whole life of God made man is beyond the reach of human reason. Without Revelation's support, our intelligence would never be able to grasp it fully or discover how well-founded it is. To human wisdom, the Incarnation remains madness, the very greatest folly.

What are the consequences of this for the ascetic? It means that he, too, if he wants to be consistent with himself, must in the eyes of the world seem to be like a madman. He will remain unaffected by the biting criticisms of a world bent on pleasure, because his madness is completely justified by Christ's madness. The example of a humiliated God gives him no choice, and so the ascetic experiences a pressing need to follow Jesus in humility. Trying to justify his attitude in any other way would be absurd. How can one appeal to natural reason to make sense of St Benedict, when he tells the monk that he should look upon himself as the last and least of all? If reason, lacking the light of faith, is one's only guide, it is impossible to convince oneself that one is last and least of all; indeed, a very superficial comparison of our talents with other people's will convince us that the contrary is true. But Jesus' example leads us to an altogether different conclusion: by coming to dwell among us sinners, the Redeemer took no account of his true dignity, he emptied and renounced himself, "He did not regard equality with God as something to be grasped, but emptied himself, taking the form of a servant" (Phil. 2:6-7). So, in order to follow this example which has been set for him, the ascetic will always take the last place, firmly convinced that this is right for anyone who wishes to follow Christ.

* * *

The second stage of Christ's divine pilgrimage finds concrete expression in his stay on earth, "I came into the world."

Jesus' earthly life was one of obedience and sacrifice, he came to obey and suffer — but why impose such a cruel destiny on oneself? Undoubtedly to show us the greatness of his love: love is shown in suffering. In suffering, you show your faithfulness to your friend and the sincerity of your love. The greatest love and charity is shown by going as far as to lay down your life for your friend. Our Lord gave us the clearest possible evidence of his infinite love by submitting himself, for our sakes, to the most terrible tortures and a shameful death.

Another reason could be added: in order to give us an example of every virtue and teach us, in a very special way, patience and serenity amidst the most difficult circumstances.

These reasons make sufficient sense, but do not supply the ultimate reason for the fact that, throughout his life, Jesus showed an unvarying preference for suffering. We need a different starting point: reparation. The Redeemer came on earth to destroy sin, to submit himself to its deadly consequences and to free us from them. With that goal, he submitted himself to the will of the Heavenly Father who had decreed death as the penalty for sin. Certainly, he could have freed us in a thousand other ways, and without even the appearance of suffering, but in order to fulfil the will which had so decreed, Christ did not reject terrible and demeaning punishment. To snatch mankind from Satan's power and undergo the punishment laid down by God for traitors, those were the main motives for the Redeemer's decision to immolate himself, humiliated on a gibbet. His precious blood was the most effective reparation for Adam's disobedience.

As we saw, Jesus' "I came from the Father" led to the development of *xeniteia*, pilgrimage and *stenochoria*; it is the root of silence, humility, contempt of self; then, "I have come into the world" explains the necessity of suffering and mortification. We will deal with these subjects, which are so important for the ascetic life, at greater length in the next chapter, which will also bring out the relationship which unites mortification to martyrdom and enlisting under Jesus Christ in their common battle against the demon.

Jesus' "I have come into the world" also shows us the necessity of obedience. The ascetic who follows in Jesus Christ's footsteps is not following his own natural inclinations. St Nilus says, "As you have learned from Jesus Christ, you are to march with him, obeying one another. He was obedient to the Father, even unto death, even death on the cross, and this is the measure he laid down for our obedience."[13]

The Rule of St Benedict also derives obedience from imitation of Christ. According to St Benedict, perfect obedience befits those who prefer nothing to the love of Christ (RB 5). In the same passage, speaking of obedience, he says, "Whoever behaves like this, fulfils the Lord's precept: 'I did not come to do my own will, but the will of Him who sent me'." Obedience practised in imitation of our Lord has two characteristics: it is unhesitating and pleases God and men. Obedience is unhesitating, because it consists of complete renunciation of self-will. Jesus Christ did not do his own will, but his Father's. The ascetic shapes himself to that model when he does not live according to the judgements of his own reason and the desires of his self-will, but follows the monastic Rule which he has taken up and the training of his spiritual Father. Obedience, furthermore, is pleasing to men, welcomed by them. In all his behaviour, the acetic opposes his superior in nothing, he shapes himself to Jesus' behaviour, and Jesus' attitude could never be other than pleasing to men.

---

[13] Nilus, *De voluntaria paupertate* 66: PG 79, 1059B

Imitation of Christ

* * *

The ascetic, then, by following the way which Jesus trod, acts as he did, as a humble and obedient pilgrim. As we saw, these aspects of ascetic life originate in the first two stages of the way Christ followed. Imitation of the third stage—the return to the Father—is very closely linked to the importance of prayer in the ascetic's life, and we will speak of that later.

Now let us see how imitation of Jesus Christ is fulfilled in the man himself. It is not confined to a moral imitation, a conformity of his own actions to those of Jesus, as might be true of our imitation of the saints or of heroes in general. Imitation of Christ goes further, because it implies a true and physical union with the Lord through sanctifying grace. Whoever imitates a saint, or some man or other, is united to him by a moral tie, whereas the Christian and ascetic who imitate the Lord truly unite themselves to him, in a physical way.

True union with Jesus Christ is, as we know, the effect of sanctifying grace, which makes us members of his mystical body. This incorporation lays the foundation and supplies the means for his imitation. Let us go into this a little deeper.

When we speak of sanctifying grace, we need to exclude any ideas of this supernatural gift that are too static. Grace unites us to Jesus Christ, to his person, and simultaneously makes us sharers in his death. Sacred Scripture uses two images to describe our real union with Jesus Christ, the vine and union with the mystical Body of Jesus Christ. Some people say that these two doctrines express the same truth, and others again, who think Paul's teaching about the body and its members is simultaneously too vague and too bold, prefer the Johannine symbol of vine and branches, but careful examination shows that there are some elements in St Paul's teaching which cannot be found in St John.

"I am the vine, you are the branches" (Jn. 15:5). This idea is much used nowadays to help people understand our union with the mystic Christ and explain its beneficial influence on the faithful. It is, however, important to avoid the exaggeration of those who would limit this to the positive and consoling aspect, that of our own "divinization". In our present situation, in order to become holy, we cannot leave the cross and mortification out of the picture. Hence the need to refer to the doctrine of the (mystical) Body of Christ. Comparing Jesus to the vine and ourselves to the branches certainly brings out the continuing and vital influence of Christ on the faithful. Separation from Christ would be the same as cutting ourselves off from the source of divine life, which would mean spiritual death. All that can be found in the doctrine of the mystical Body. The faithful are united to Jesus in one living organism, they are given life by one and the same spirit, guided by the same head, each playing their own parts and with their own responsibilities. More, this doctrine expresses our duty to imitate Jesus Christ. The members of the Body of Christ must share the lot of Christ's humanity. Head and members make up a perfect unity and share fully in their destiny: a single person, a single destiny. That is complete union with Jesus Christ, that is the deepest meaning of imitation of Christ. The Christian who has been allowed to share the lot of Jesus Christ is destined not only to the Passion and the Cross, but also to his glorious Resurrection and Ascension. It is quite clear that the theme of vine and branches cannot express all that our union with Jesus brings about.

The ascetic life is then an imitation of Jesus Christ, a truth which has brought us to the doctrine of the body of Christ, the theological expression of that imitation, and which is first brought about in baptism and the Eucharist. Here is an appropriate moment to say something about its importance in the ascetic life.

Baptized into the death of Jesus Christ, the Christian dies with him through baptism (Rom. 6:23), imitating and following Jesus in death. Through the Eucharist, food and nourishment of his new life, the faithful shares mystically in the sacrifice, the Resurrection and the Ascension of the Redeemer. We do not propose here to go into the theological teaching on these two sacraments. It should be enough to recall that by receiving the Eucharist, the Christian is more closely united to Christ glorified, and is transformed and glorified with him. Such is the deep meaning of that classical theological teaching, that the Eucharist is spiritual nourishment, which is not transformed into the one

Imitation of Christ

who receives it, but which rather transforms the recipient into itself. In Eucharistic communion the Christian is absorbed into Christ, and in Christ is a sharer in the world's liberation from sin, and in some sense shares in his Ascension and heavenly Glorification. It is true to say that through the Eucharist, the Christian anticipates the future life of glory.

Baptism and the Eucharist, then, sacramentally bring about the imitation of Jesus Christ: they make us sharers in his destiny, as St Paul requires of all the members of the mystical Body. One could rightly call them the ascetic's sacraments, because they lay the foundations of the ascetic life. Baptism lays the foundation on which the whole of the ascetic's life is built.

Baptism is death to sin and to the world, but in reality, nonetheless, it is only the principal of sin that dies in our soul, sin's consequences remain, and in particular concupiscence, and that is why our body is still called "sinful flesh". The ascetic's life sets out to destroy sin by neutralising its consequences in us. Only one word can synthesize the entire task of the ascetic: "mortification", putting to death all those leanings which to a greater or lesser degree are infected by sin.

This is the underlying reason why monastic profession, the solemn consecration of a man to the ascetic life, can be called a "second baptism". Saying that does not represent a claim that profession is a sort of sacrament that can free from sin, *ex opere operato*, by the deed itself. It simply means that the act of charity involved in the spontaneous renunciation of self-will and consecration to the service of God not merely purifies the soul from every stain of sin but also brings the effects of the act of baptism to perfection. By his profession, the monk abandons the world, even in externals: he breaks all the ties which might hold him back, publicly, before the altar and in the presence of his monastic family, he makes the irrevocable decision to eliminate all compromise with sin, to renounce all the joys of this world, even those that are good and licit, and to lead a life of perpetual mortification and denial. That is why monastic profession is truly a second baptism, a complement to the first death undergone with Christ in baptism, and why the profession ceremony is full of allusions to mystical death.

CHRISTIAN ASCETICISM

The Eucharist has a different relationship to the ascetic life. It is, as we said, essentially a sharing in the sacrifice of the Cross and in the Resurrection and Ascension, a sacramental anticipation of the life to come. It is a constant support—the ascetic, a feeble creature, might tire of his life of mortification and be overcome. The Eucharist supplies the necessary strength, union with Jesus Christ in his sacrifice welds the ascetic's effort to the Master's universal sacrifice. The creature's humble and painful efforts undergo a quite special transformation and acquire an absolute value in union with Jesus Christ's sacrifice. They share in the great work of the Redemption, because, through their union to the head of the mystical Body, they enjoy the privileges won by Jesus Christ's sacrifice. Sharing in the Resurrection and the Ascension, which sharing in the Eucharist implies, is a constant foretaste of the eternal reward, which this mystery allows us truly to enjoy, albeit in a way that is hidden and inaccessible to our senses. The monk and the ascetic are dead to the world, but the Eucharist makes them sharers in the glorious life of Jesus Christ—they are dead, certainly, but they are already living another life, which has nothing to do with earthly life, they are living the heavenly life. Like angels in a mortal body, they seem to live in heaven and enjoy now the glories of the future life.

Those who viewed the Christian ascetics as dwellers in another world, as angels of God having nothing to do with human life's changes, were not wrong. Like the angels, citizens of heaven, their part is to sing the glories and the praises of God around the throne of the Most High. This goes to show how the ascetic life, as imitation of Jesus Christ, founded on a real sharing in his destiny by means of the sacraments, can be both a second death and an anticipation of the glory to come.

* * *

This conception of the ascetic life as an imitation of Christ founded on a real transformation of ourselves through the sacraments can help us to grasp other aspects of it.

First of all, the fact that ascetic life and monastic life are simply the logical outcome and the perfect fulfilment of "ordinary" Christian life, if one can put it that way. What we mean by that expression is the sort of life to which every Christian is bound who wishes to be saved, for there can be no Christian life without imitation of Jesus Christ — the very name "Christian" demonstrates that the faithful belong to Christ. The source of the ordinary Christian's life, nourishment and growth are in the sacraments of Jesus. By baptismal promises, the Christian solemnly promises to consecrate himself to imitation of Christ, to follow his example, to do all that He asks of him. Ascetic life does no more than follow this abandonment through to its ultimate consequences. The ascetic separates himself more completely from the world and renounces even what is permitted.

Christianity is not a two-track morality, one for the ordinary Christian, the other for the ascetic. Both share the same morality, the same rule of life, but the ascetic life observes the counsels as well as obeying the commandments. Monks and ascetics are not more Christian than others, all are imitators of Jesus Christ, each in their own way. Ascetic life is not part of the hierarchy, as are the diaconate and the priesthood. Although the consecration conferred on the monk is often called his ordination, it does not confer any indelible character on him in the way that priestly ordination does. What sets the ascetic above the ordinary Christian is based on his personal ascetic activity, a more perfect fulfilment of the Christian life, a more complete development of the supernatural way of life given in baptism. The monk's dignity, unlike that of the priest, does not depend on his having received ordination, but on his ascetic zeal. The priest, once validly ordained, remains so for ever, whatever he does, and so is always capable of priestly and consecratory actions; he possesses forever the priestly dignity, even if he is personally unworthy of it. The monk, on the other hand, by the mere fact of his profession of the ascetic life, objectively possesses neither dignity nor indelible character nor any special power, but is under obligation to lead a life of ascesis and mortification. The difference between him and the ordinary Christian is proportionate to the degree of love with which he has consecrated himself to that kind of life and to the degree of love with which he lives it out. That is why any claim to special dignity would be strictly opposed to humility, the fundamental virtue of ascetic life.

CHRISTIAN ASCETICISM

Even though the ascetic life and the ordinary Christian life coincide in various aspects, they nonetheless remain distinct, though the distinction does not result from the ascetic having a special rank in the hierarchy: ascetic life is a "charism". Tradition ranks the ascetic life among the charismatic gifts. St Cyril of Jerusalem, after having listed the well-known charisms given by the Holy Spirit, adds, "In one, the Holy Spirit strengthens temperance, to another he teaches what leads to mercy, and to another still, he gives the gifts of fasting and practising the exercises of the ascetic life."[14] If the ascetic life is a charism, then it is not open to all, but only to those called to it in a special way by God's grace.

* * *

The charismatic nature of the ascetic life highlights some of its other properties. Charisms are caused by the Holy Spirit, whose gifts are abundantly poured out on the Christian members of the messianic kingdom. Therefore, it is the Holy Spirit who makes this life possible, by giving the necessary strength to those who submit to it. A life which, from a natural point of view might seem impossible on account of its more than human demands, becomes possible for one in whom the Spirit of God dwells and fills with divine strength. This shows a link between the ascetic life and martyrdom. Like martyrdom, the ascetic life, the final outcome of the Christian life, is a particular manifestation of the Spirit, which enables the achievement of what seems impossible to nature. The ascetic can rightly claim that if his weakness is upheld by the Spirit, it is only to enable such a life of mortification and self-denial.

Every charism shows the Spirit as Consoler. It is truly comforting for good Christians living in the world to be able to see and admire the austere, mortified lives of ascetics. It makes them feel stimulated to bear their crosses and privations, and in their troubles and sorrows they are consoled by knowing that the brothers are interceding and praying to the Lord for

---

14   Cyril of Jerusalem, Mystagogical Catechesis, 16, 12; *The Writings of St. Cyril of Jerusalem*, Vol. 2, translated by Leo P. McCauley, S. J. and Anthony A. Stephenson, FOTC Vol. 64 (CUA Press 1970), p. 82.

them, their needs and their salvation, day and night. The lives of ascetics who deserve the name and honour their profession is an example for others and a constant exhortation to patience and perseverance, a constant reminder that a truly Christian life without trials and sufferings is inconceivable.

The charismatic character of the ascetic life also shows that it is a truly supernatural way of life, no one may launch themselves into it unless called by the Lord and clothed with the power of the Spirit. That it is a supernatural life means that it goes beyond reason's limitations and that a purely natural sociology is inadequate to account for it—indeed, as already pointed out, such an attempt would be an error, running the risk of denigrating the ascetic life.

All the charisms are an integral part of the Christian society which is the Body of Christ; if a Christian claimed exclusive ownership of a charism, he would no longer be a member of the one body. In a body, each member exists, lives and works for the others, and so the ascetic life must be useful to the community. It would be a misunderstanding of the ascetic and monastic life if one thought it consisted of speculations and contemplations useful only to the individual seeking perfection and personal sanctification. Nor is a purely natural usefulness the goal. Every ascetic, the desert hermit and the cloistered monk, devoted to a purely contemplative life serves the whole community through his life of mortification and prayer. One should not forget that in the life of the Church, the spread of the Gospel depends more on God's grace than human effort. Grace is not conditional on our merit, but it is often in accordance with God's will to grant it in response to the prayers and intercession of his friends and of the saints, hence Pius XI's insistence on the need for and usefulness of the life of ascetic contemplation. It is also true that nowadays, even in the heart of the Church itself, such ideas are not valued as they should be, a fact which shows that now, more than ever, it is necessary to orient ourselves to a supernatural view, and a life founded on such principles.

Although monks have made themselves useful to the Church and to society in numerous sacred and profane disciplines, and this fits in with the lives of cenobites who have retained more connections to the world than hermits, such merits are purely secondary. The ministry of charity, to which the monk chiefly devotes himself by prayer, is altogether more important, for that is in accord with the nature of his charism. Others exercise charity by a variety of external works, which they have been called by God to provide for the good of the whole Body. St Augustine said, "Christ taught the Apostles how to follow where he had preceded, 'I give you a new commandment,' he said, 'that you love one another.' These are the steps we must take to follow Christ."[15] Each must practise charity in the situation and in the way which God has fixed, and in this way follow and imitate Christ.

The ascetic imitates the Lord, intensifying the work of mortification which baptism began, he is in essence a penitent. No ascetic life can be separated from works of penance. The Rule of its very self is ordered to the ascetic life, since its rigorous observance is, just on its own, a sufficiently toilsome penance, and on top of that are added the mortifications to which each feels moved by grace and with the approval of his spiritual director. All Christians living in the world rightly think that the ascetic life — and by that, they especially mean the monks — is a constant mortification. It is true that this spirit of mortification has often disappeared from monasteries, as history frequently shows, but this lack was not limited to the cloister, but overflowed and spread throughout the Church. Weak human nature, fond of a comfortable life, is too inclined to forget and neglect this fact. The ascetic may let himself be drawn into worldly ease, which bit by bit may permanently take him from the life to which he consecrated himself.

There are plenty of theological arguments around, which attempt to falsify the penitential ideal of ascesis. Some make use of the principle, "Grace builds on nature". "If you want to lead a spiritual life which is sound and built on grace," they say, "you must take care of your body and be in good health, and do nothing which might go against nature." It is true that

---

15 Augustine, *On John*, 64, 4, (3); *Tractates on the Gospel of John 55–111*, translated by John W. Rettig, FOTC Vol. 90 (CUA Press 1994), p. 273.

Imitation of Christ

one can overdo penance, monastic history shows the truth of that, but that does not exempt from the law of penance which remains in force for every ascetic. The saints have always shown ingenuity in finding new mortifications, especially when poor health or other external obstacles prevented them from performing greater penitential acts.

Sometimes people distinguish penitential Orders from the others; it is well to be clear about what this means, because it is a contradiction in terms to speak of monks or ascetics without penance. The distinction might be justified only if some Order gave greater importance than another to acts of penance, but even so, the difference is one of degree and is not essential.

In imitation of Christ, the ascetic empties himself through a life of mortification. This mystical death is a consequence of the ascetic life, dying to all that is of the world. The Lives of the ancient monks show the logical way they put this into practice. They tell, for example, of Abba Arsenius, to whom one day government officials came with the will of a friend who had been a Senator, and who had left to Arsenius a large part of his estate. The Abba gave them back the will and sent them away, saying, "He has only just died, but I died long ago."

* * *

A final thought sums up all we have said about the ascetic life as an imitation of Christ: the idea of risk.

Whoever is approaching death must abandon everything. Following Christ's example, the ascetic renounces himself completely, gives himself to Christ, to be incorporated into him, identified with him and truly bind his destiny to Christ's. Human nature trembles at the thought, for embracing the ascetic life entails risking the body's life; there is also the risk that you will not be able to follow your own inclinations, even good ones, you risk everything. This uncertainty gives birth to a certain anxiety and to sadness. Mystical death, like physical death, is preceded by an agony, a struggle, but the Lord's word consoles and strengthens us, "Blessed are those who mourn, for they will be comforted" (Mt. 5:4).

CHRISTIAN ASCETICISM

* * *

The ascetic life does not oblige the ascetic and the monk alone: it is also obligatory for the priest, and so the monk who is a priest is doubly obliged. The ascetic life of the monk, even the most contemplative, and the priestly life, are not opposed in this. The priest who celebrates holy Mass must make this sacrifice his, in every aspect of his life. The bishop explicitly reminds him of this in the ordination rite,

> Know what you are doing, imitate what you touch. You are celebrating the mystery of the Lord's death, and you must therefore seek to mortify your members by keeping far away from every vice and every concupiscence. May the sweet odour of your life be the delight of the Church of Jesus Christ, so that by your word and example you may build up that house which is the family of God.

This teaching of the imitation of Christ bears out the portrait of the ascetic given in the first chapter: the ascetic separates from the world and overcomes it, just as Jesus Christ did. The seed of this victorious imitation is conferred by the sacrament of baptism, and whoever truly wishes to imitate Jesus Christ must develop and grow this seed. There is only one way to reach the total perfection of the Christian life, only one way which really works: penance and mystical death. No one who has not decided to act in accord with this has the right to call himself an ascetic. Jesus Christ crucified is our only way, and no one can come to the Father, except through Christ.

CHAPTER 4

The Ascetic as Martyr

THE ASCETIC SEPARATES FROM THE world in order to follow and imitate Jesus Christ, not by a merely moral imitation, but a primarily real and physical imitation, which in baptism begins by sharing in Christ's Passion and which personal ascesis perfects.

In a quite special way, bloody martyrdom is an imitation of Christ, but so is the non-bloody martyrdom of the ascetic, and there is a very close affinity between monastic life and martyrdom.

Scripture itself teaches us that martyrdom is not just an imitation of Christ, but its most perfect imitation: "Therefore be imitators of God, as beloved children," St Paul tells the Ephesians. "And walk in love, as Christ loved us and gave himself up for us, a fragrant offering and sacrifice to God" (Eph. 5:1–2). Christ, our great model, offered his life for his friends. To love unto death, that is the rule for whoever would follow him. St Peter says the same, "For to this you have been called, because Christ also suffered for you, leaving you an example, so that you should follow in his steps" (1 Pet. 2:21). St Augustine relates martyrdom to the Eucharist when commenting on this text, and he goes on,

> The martyrs most zealously fulfilled this [relationship between martyrdom and the Eucharist]. If we do not want to celebrate their memory in vain, and if we wish to approach that table at which they were fed, then we too must also prepare ourselves in the same way. They showed such great charity that the Lord himself says that it cannot be exceeded. They behaved towards their brethren as they had learned at the table of the Lord.[1]

According to St Augustine, the martyrs truly followed the example that Jesus Christ left us. For them, sharing in the Eucharist meant, in a very concrete way, Jesus' example of

---

1 Augustine, *On John* 84, 1, (3); *Tractates on the Gospel of John 55–111*, translated by John W. Rettig, FOTC Vol. 90 (CUA Press 1994), p. 134.

CHRISTIAN ASCETICISM

offering himself for his brothers and giving them the strength necessary for the fulfilment of that act of heroic love.

We too share in the same table, and this thought ought constantly to arouse us to follow their example whenever circumstances demand it.

From the apostolic era onwards, martyrdom was recognized as a perfect imitation of Jesus Christ, and very soon there was talk of replacing martyrdom with an equivalent, especially once the persecutions ended and it became less frequent. The possibility of another kind of death was put forward. If henceforth there would be no possibility of suffering the kind of death which separates soul from body for Christ's sake, might it be possible to inflict on oneself another kind of death, separating the soul, the spiritual being, from the passions of the flesh? This, according to a very ancient tradition, is the martyrdom of Christian ascetics.

In the *Life of St Antony*, we are told that he came to Alexandria to seek martyrdom during the persecution, because, as a tried and tested hermit, he could not forget the Church's needs. He did not spontaneously give himself up to the persecutors, an action which the Church has always regarded as blameworthy temerity, but openly exhorted and strengthened the Christians everywhere, without a shadow of fear. Not having been granted the martyrdom of blood, his biographer tells us, he returned to his poor cell, "And there, by every day contending in the battles of the faith, he was a martyr in his conscience."[2] Another testimony from the same era tells,

> The martyrs often achieved perfection in one short contest. But the life of a monk, a daily struggle for Jesus, is also martyrdom. It is not merely a struggle against flesh and blood, but against the principalities, the powers and the masters of the world of darkness, against the evil spirits. This struggle must go on to the last breath, and then the combatants, wearing the armour of God, will receive their crown.[3]

---

[2] Athanasius, *Life of Antony* 47; Ancient Christian Writers, No. 10, Newly translated and annotated by Robert T. Meyer, Ph. D., Newman Press, New York, N.Y./ Mahwah, N.J., 1950 & 1978, p. 60.

[3] Antony the Monk, known as Melissa (PG 136, 1113), *Sentences collected*

The Ascetic as Martyr

We run no risk of being wrong in stating that a very solid tradition regards the ascetic and monastic life as a martyrdom, and the reason for this is clear—they are both imitations of Jesus Christ, both fulfil God's command to Abraham, "Go from your country and your kindred" (Gen. 12:1). Each does so in its own way, the martyr leaves the world definitively, by sacrificing his own life, while monks and ascetics mortify their natural inclinations by detaching themselves, even physically, from them, truly sacrificing their most legitimate desires. Ascetic tradition applies this text from Genesis to both of them, for they both obey the same command: separate yourself from the world following the example of Jesus Christ, who was the very first to withdraw himself from the devil's power and free himself from the world in order to return to the Father.

These facts are indicative of the close relationship between the ascetic life and martyrdom, but there are others which seem opposed to a too-close linking, and we should not ignore these. The primary difference between martyrdom and the ascetic life is that the former is a bloody imitation of Jesus Christ's example. We should not forget that no one may confront martyrdom by their own choice, whereas the ascetic life is a voluntary and deliberate imitation of Christ. In it, more than in martyrdom, personal decision comes first, even though the ascetic life also presupposes a special vocation and God's grace. But these differences should not be regarded too lightly, and we should not forget how closely they are related. Let us go on to make this more clear.

* * *

If we want a better understanding of the ascetic's and the monk's place in the Church, we need first to understand the martyr's place in the Church. Two characteristics distinguish the martyr: he "confesses" and is a "friend" of Jesus Christ.

The martyr confesses Christ: his faith testifies to him before men. Through the martyr's profession of faith, Christ receives a certain amount of publicity in the eyes of the world. That is what St Augustine meant, when he wrote of the Apostles,

---

from sacred and profane authors: Athanasius.

Jesus Christ wanted to make them his martyrs, which means witnesses, through the action of the Holy Spirit. Through the work of the Holy Spirit, they would endure persecutions and all sorts of trials, and enkindled with that divine fire, maintain the fervour of charity needed for preaching.[4]

Jesus chose the apostles to make himself known and to spread his teaching throughout the whole world. In St Augustine's view, that is equivalent to martyrdom. Obviously, preaching Jesus Christ in this way does not come naturally to every propagandist or master-teacher. Rather, it demands more than natural strength; it needs the Holy Spirit. The act of confessing Jesus Christ is inseparable from contradiction and persecution by the world; indeed, one could even say that such is almost the natural environment for its growth. That is not surprising, since it is about preaching a crucified God, which is madness in the eyes of the world. Martyrdom, then, is so to speak the normal way of publicizing Jesus and Christianity in the only way which suits the intention of the divine Founder. In martyrdom, usually, this heroic testimony is called forth and punished by official organisms of the State and public life, the authorities themselves officially confront the martyr. Through martyrdom, Christ steadfastly affirms that his religion is not a private institution or sect, but a true society with the right to grow, and which forces human authority to come to a decision about it. The problem it poses concerns society itself.

Seen from this point of view, the person of the martyr takes on a universal character which goes beyond personal interest and makes the martyr a champion facing human authority. This is why such a confession demands an act of complete renunciation, because his own interests are subordinated to Christ's. At the end of time, the scale of values will be upset, and human authority will no longer be permitted to condemn or oppress Christians. In a verdict without appeal, the Father will manifest his Reign and decide who are to be members of his Kingdom, and then the

---

4 Augustine, *On John* (1); *Tractates on the Gospel of John 55-111*, translated by John W. Rettig, FOTC Vol. 90 (CUA Press 1994), p. 182.

martyr who was trampled underfoot for Christ's glory will hear from Christ himself the most consoling speech in his defence, "So everyone who acknowledges me before men, I also will acknowledge before my Father who is in heaven" (Mt. 10:32). Thus, the martyr, by his confession before men, has merited the right to enter the Kingdom. Persecutions have snatched him from this world, this world's judges have denied him the right to exist in society, but Jesus Christ has reserved a place of honour for him in the Kingdom of his Father, in the glorious company of eternal life.

Martyrdom is thus the Christian religion's most solemn way of laying claim to its right to public life. Martyrdom would not be possible without this religion-based claim. Human society in which purely natural principles reign, normally views such a profession of faith as no more than madness and pretentiousness, so conflict is inevitable and necessarily ends in the martyr's sacrifice, in the world's view, a sad and disastrous end, but in the sight of the angels a joyful and glorious end.

Further, martyrdom has always been considered as the highest form of sanctity and the most perfect fulfilment of the path set out for the Christian. It is therefore clear that a similar conflict, if not on the same scale, is imposed on the conscience of every Christian, for no one can escape it or take refuge in a spot where no one can see him; there will never be reasons lacking which oblige him to commit himself and, one way or another, bear witness to Christ before men. When a large percentage of those under its governance profess that religion, it makes no sense for the state to try to ignore the Christian religion and to claim to limit it to matters of private conscience alone.

So it is that the martyr affirms one of the most precious fundamental truths of Christianity: he demonstrates its public character; the martyr preaches Jesus Christ before the world, becoming a spectacle to God and his angels, because this public element of martyrdom is not limited to this earth alone, since it is only one part of the world. Every martyrdom is a great drama unfolding in the sight of men, and before God and his angels, it is only one small aspect of that constant struggle (even if it is sometimes less bitter than at others) waged between the Reign of God and the enemy powers which govern this world.

This explains why every persecution of the Church, whether it be universal and directed against the whole Christian world, or whether it be limited to a single individual, has something devilish about it. The tortures are every time the same, because the testimony the martyr gives and the struggle endured it is not a matter of man-to-man combat, but a contest between God and the enemy powers. And so it is the strength given by the Holy Spirit which enables the martyr to confess the faith, even amidst the worst of cruelties, just as it is the Adversary, the devil, who is acting in the persecutor. Who will have the final victory in this contest? It is easy to guess, and the martyrs themselves, illuminated by the Holy Spirit, saw clearly against whom they were fighting. During her martyrdom, St Perpetua said, "I realized that I had to battle against demons, not against wild beasts. All the same, I knew I would be victorious." By martyrdom the Christian religion both demonstrates and acquires its public character. Martyrdom reveals clearly what the Christian life is, and what is its situation in this world. For whoever wants to rule his life in accord with the teachings of Jesus Christ, conflict is inevitable, for in a world like ours the Christian life cannot flourish in peace, it will be a struggle to the very end.

The martyr is also a friend of Jesus Christ. A friend is the opposite of a servant. The Apostles were not Christ's servants, but his friends, and indeed they shared his confidences and enjoyed intimacy with him. The martyrs, too, are friends; they are so pleasing to God that the gate of Paradise is opened to them immediately. On this subject, a most ancient tradition tells how the souls of the other saints have to wait at Heaven's gate until the end of time — a belief that is now inadmissible. The basis for this privilege is the very close union of the martyrs with Jesus Christ, that they show by their perfect imitation of the Saviour. As the words of the good thief show, it is he himself who admits souls to Paradise, "Today you shall be with me in Paradise" (Lk. 23:42). The friend of Jesus Christ has freedom of speech, *parresia*. He can tell his friend all his desires and requests, and by the mere fact of so doing, is very likely to be heard. This union of the martyr with Jesus Christ is so intimate that it establishes a special presence of Christ in the very soul of the martyr.

The Ascetic as Martyr

The union with the Saviour which every one of the faithful possesses reaches its highest degree in the martyr. This altogether special presence gives the strength to endure every adversity, not in our human person and by reason of it, but as a member of something higher, namely the mystical Body of Jesus Christ. The Acts of the martyrs emphasize this point; they tell of dialogues between Jesus Christ and his martyr during the tortures, and of Jesus Christ who leads the martyr, freed from his body, to Paradise. This union with Christ shows that the martyr is already interiorly in the other world, even though, during his torments, he remains earth-bound. So it is not the man alone who undergoes the suffering, any more than it is he alone, with his poor limited understanding, who replies to the loaded interrogations of the persecutors; no, it is Jesus Christ who lives and acts with him and in him. The martyr who is so closely united to his divine friend becomes, by the very fact of this intimacy, a mediator for other Christians, who can use him as an intermediary for their requests in the hope of being more surely heard.

The martyr's confession is a real "consolation" for the faithful in affliction, who are sometimes so anguished and feeble; it shows the invincible power of faith and how faithful Jesus Christ is in carrying out his promises. For unbelievers, martyrdom testifies to the Church's invincibility and the meek and patient Christ's irresistible power, and to the entirely supernatural and interior life of his Kingdom.

Witness to Christ and friend of Christ, the martyr can never be lacking in the Church. In every age, it must be possible to find in her bosom those who confess Christ, whose confession shows each new generation what the Church is: the continuation of the work begun by Jesus Christ himself in his glorious Passion, and in his battle against the devil. That is why the Passion will never be absent from the members of that Church, any more than will be the combat with the devil, using the same weapons that Jesus our King used: patience and suffering.

The Church also always needs people who are specially chosen friends of Jesus, friends in whom he is present in a quite special way. These friends are not strangers to us, for they know what are the Church's present needs, and they place them before Christ.

Being a martyr, then, is a specific vocation, an extraordinary gift of God. God may so choose to dignify anyone, and any Christian life may end in this way. Priests, however, should be especially ready to confess Jesus Christ, as St Augustine points out,

> The Good Shepherd lays down his life for his sheep, so that they may be his witnesses. Should not those to whom Christ has entrusted his sheep to feed and instruct therefore battle for the truth, even to the shedding of their blood and till death?[5]

* * *

Now we need to see how these characteristics of Christ's martyr apply to the ascetic, whom we have so often compared to the martyr, and see how well they fit the ascetic. This will enable us to grasp the close relationship which links martyrdom and the ascetic life, and to see how important it is for the Church. We have already said that both martyrdom and the ascetic life have in common the fact that they are both a perfect imitation of Jesus Christ. The martyr and the ascetic separate themselves completely from the world, from their country and from their goods. Like martyrdom, the ascetic life's primary demand is mortification, which in the martyr's case always takes the same shape, though admittedly the manner may differ considerably, because there are different ways of suffering, but if it is genuine martyrdom, it always ends in death. No real martyr can avoid that, because, without death, the dignity of martyrdom does not exist, and from this aspect there is no difference between a martyr of our own era and a martyr of the first two centuries.

Real mortification is also the norm for the ascetic life; if the ascetic life is to be a martyrdom, it cannot be so without mortification, otherwise it would have changed its nature, it would be something else, and all that would remain of the ascetic life would be the name — it would be as much of a contradiction as martyrdom without death. Even though the outward framework of life may have completely changed, the twentieth-century

---

[5] Augustine, *On John* 123, 5: *Tractates on the Gospel of John 112–124*, translated by John W. Rettig, FOTC Vol. 92 (CUA Press 1994), p. 80.

The Ascetic as Martyr

ascetic can be no different from the ascetic of the primitive Church in this respect. The acetic cannot compromise with the world on this matter, nor adapt to changed times. That would be a real betrayal, apostasy from his true vocation. One might object that maybe our age no longer has the same mental outlook, and so cannot bear even the slightest reference to "mortification". Nonetheless, the ideal of the ascetic life must remain essentially unchanged, just as the ideal of martyrdom. With the passage of time, the external appearances of the ascetic life may change, but it must nonetheless always remain a real imitation of the sufferings of Christ. It would be a strange failing in logic to subtract this characteristic, and claim to lead an ascetic life without mortification. It would be much better to change one's way of life than to find oneself faced with such an incredible contradiction as an ascetic life without mortification.

Both the ascetic and the martyr are combatants, the one by a mortified life and the other by suffering unto death. For the ascetic, being a combatant does not necessarily mean defending himself and attacking the Church's enemies by what he writes or says; the primary meaning of the term is spiritual, and the battle is primarily against the passions and sin. Just as the devil's chief weapons against the ascetic are the passions, so he uses external persecutors to destroy the Christian life. Physical death testifies to the martyr's final, decisive victory over the devil, who has failed to prevent him confessing Jesus Christ. Through death he has reached perfect union with his Redeemer. The ascetic's victory is to be won by means of the mystical life and by means of overcoming even the worst temptations, by never separating himself from Jesus Christ for empty pleasures. That is mystical death; his final victory over the devil will be marked by his persevering to the end.

This, you see, is how martyrs and ascetic resemble one another: they both die for Christ. On account of that likeness, the ascetic also in some sense acquires the other dignities of the martyr: he becomes a friend of Jesus Christ, a spiritual man, a mediator, someone who intercedes for his brothers. This role as mediator and intercessor is as much of the essence of his life as it is of the martyr's, a grave obligation for him and is his means of practising charity.

The ascetic's primary charitable action is prayer for others, intercession, and should never be lacking in any ascetic life. The martyr renounces all future activity, but through martyrdom and death becomes his brothers' greatest spiritual benefactor, and his very death sets him in the best place for this. The same is true of the ascetic, who is also primarily a spiritual benefactor. His vocation obliges him to be a man of prayer and intercession. The priestly dignity and other obligations which accompany it may be added to his ascetic vocation, as also the call to the apostolate, but without ever over-riding the fundamental, essential obligation to exercise charity through prayer. In its absence, one may be a priest, an apostle or even a man of action, but one cannot be an ascetic.

The ascetic is necessary to the Church for the same reason as the martyr, but is specially needed during times of peace. In time of persecution, the martyr is there, publicly confessing Christ and his teaching, making it clear as daylight that the Church is essentially the suffering Body of Christ. In more peaceful times, that task falls to the ascetic, for when there is a relatively good relationship between human authority and the Church, when there are no martyrs, when the general tranquillity of the times seems to invite a going with the flow of worldly life and its advantages, then the ascetic life becomes more necessary. Then is the time for the ascetic to show, through an austere, detached life, through contempt for worldly dignities and goods, what is the real relationship of the Church to the world. Lastly, the ascetic is a living symbol for those Christians who cannot find perfect peace in the world, showing them that we are not of this world; his life of struggle against passions and temptations shows more clearly that the Christian life is a constant struggle; and that even when externally all is well and relations with human authorities are good, excellent and altogether on the best of terms, the Church can never definitively root herself here below, for until the coming like a thunderclap of the Kingdom of God, until the day of Jesus Christ's return, she will never enjoy ultimate peace. That is why, when the Church ran the danger of being too closely linked to the world, in times of "secularization", preachers and true ascetics

The Ascetic as Martyr

arose, showing everyone openly by their lives, where the limits lay. Ascetics like these take the place of martyrs, by warning and strengthening the faithful.

So the Church, in times of persecution or of relative peace, is never lacking in these generous champions who show the Church's true character: not just simply a society organized to reach a higher end, but rather the continuation of Christ's sufferings, sacrificed for the salvation of souls.

* * *

The ascetic life is also in some ways a preparation for bloody martyrdom, as we see in the life of St Antony, who, while still a hermit, thought it entirely natural, and indeed indispensable, to expose himself to danger so that he might be accepted by God as a holocaust. If, as in the case of St Antony, the ascetic life is not necessarily linked to martyrdom, it remains true that ascesis is the highest and most perfect of all preparations for martyrdom. So it is that St Clement of Alexandria himself demands that the gnostic (whose ideal he sketches out)[6] be always ready for martyrdom, thirsting to undergo it, expecting it in times of persecution. Even so, it depends on the free choice of God's grace whether or not it comes about. The ascetic life is not something apart, superimposed on to ordinary Christian life, but truly it is that same Christian life taken to its perfection, crowning its logical conclusion. All Christians must prepare themselves for martyrdom in some sense, even if not all to the same degree. On the subject of this obligation, St Thomas states,

> There is no action belonging purely to the counsels which cannot in certain cases become a precept and necessary for salvation. For there are cases in which martyrdom is not necessary for eternal salvation.... These precepts must all the same take account of the disposition of souls to conform to them.[7]

---

6 St Clement of Alexandria understands his gnostic to be the teacher of the Church. Because the gnostic has attained the closest resemblance to God that is possible for a human, he has God-given authority to teach the Church.

7 Aquinas, *Summ. theol.*, IIa IIae q 124, a 3 ad 1., *Summa theol.*, 2a2ae,

Again, in some cases, as for example if the refusal of martyrdom were to become a denial of Jesus Christ and apostasy from the faith (as might happen during a persecution), each must be prepared for the supreme sacrifice. Even if this general obligation in no way reduces the special dignity of martyrdom, it still shows that everyone should retain an awareness of the possibility that one day they might find themselves forced to go that far in order to confess their faith. The ascetic faces that possibility as a reality, concretely, since through mystical death he is preparing himself, in a much more direct and immediate way, for physical death. He would be failing in his vocation were he to remain attached to the things of this world and to earthly life.

So we see once more the built-in dynamism of the ascetic life noted earlier; there is a constant urge to an ever-higher goal. The ascetic cannot stop until he has reached complete and definitive union with Jesus Christ. If the cenobitic life, ascetic life lived in common, is indeed a preparation for the more perfect ascetic life of the hermit, there is also a more perfect and higher degree than that, the witness of blood. The martyr, whom Catholic tradition unanimously regards as the highest level of sanctity (because it is a living, most faithful example and image of Jesus Christ), remains as the authentic fulfilment towards which the ascetic and the hermit strive.

The ascetic life is a direct and practical preparation for martyrdom, and acts as a reminder that, built into every Christian life, there is the possibility of its ending in bloody sacrifice. That shows the seriousness of the Christian life. Accepting faith in Jesus Christ doesn't mean peaceful enjoyment of all the tangible blessings of divine providence and a happy banishment of all difficulties — quite the opposite. Those who settle down in this world are more likely to be able to rely on having a quiet life free of tribulation. Jesus Christ leads his disciples only by the way of the Cross towards an end which, from a purely human point of view, looks, as his own end seemed, more like a disastrous

---

q. 124, a.3., ad I, Vol. 42, Courage (2a2ae. 123–40). Latin Text, English Translation, Anthony Ross, O. P. (Edinburgh, P. G. Walsh, Edinburgh, Blackfriars 1966), p. 51.

failure than a triumphant victory. We await that victory at the end of the world, when we will be taken up with him into the glory of his Resurrection and Ascension.

* * *

Consideration of these truths should lead the Christian ascetic and the monk to the profound conviction of how seriously he should take his life and his state, which is a preparation for the most testing experience of all: martyrdom. Sacred Scripture describes martyrdom as a chalice, and that was what Our Lord himself called it, when he asked his Apostles, "Are you able to drink the cup that I am to drink?" (Mt. 20:22). In the Sacrifice of the Mass, we hold in our hands the Lord's chalice, the real and tangible memorial of his passion and death. As we said earlier, participating in this Sacrifice prepares us in a very special way for that imitation of Christ fulfilled by martyrdom, and it commits us to follow him all the way to death. Each time the priest takes the chalice in his hands to drink the precious Blood, he says, "I will take the Chalice of the Lord and call upon his name." These words could be understood as meaning: In as much as I am a disciple of Jesus Christ, and on account of the ceaseless demand for greater perfection imposed on me by the ascetic life, I am ready and willing to drink the Chalice of martyrdom with Jesus Christ my Master. *Et nomen Domini invocabo*, and I will call upon the name of the Lord, I cannot lay claim to that grace of martyrdom, I can only humbly ask for it, and I wish to accept it with a good heart and singing the glory of the Lord, as though it had really been granted to me, because the grace of Christ will also give me the strength to fulfil, if necessary, this ultimate consequence of my vocation to martyrdom.

Erroneous modern ideas are not alone in falsifying the ideal of the ascetic and monastic life, which does not consist of spiritual work, nor of supplying the spiritual and temporal needs of Christians. All that may be added as an extra, but it does not constitute its essence, which consists of a life of serious mortification and detachment. That is the common ideal of the ascetic and the martyr.

This is where the true greatness, the transcendence, of the ascetic life lies. Humanly speaking, this is not a very comforting prospect, but the true comfort and consolation are in the Lord's words, "Blessed are those who mourn, for they shall be comforted" (Mt. 5:4). The consolation comes from the thought of the future glory which the painful life of mystical death will merit for us. We can apply to the monk and to the ascetic St Augustine's words on the martyr, "Were there no pain in the death, the glory of the martyr would not be so great."[8]

---

8 Augustine, *On John*, 123, 5: *Tractates on the Gospel of John 112–124*, translated by John W. Rettig, FOTC Vol. 92 (CUA Press 1994), p. 80.

CHAPTER 5

The Soldier of Jesus Christ

THE ASCETIC LIFE IS AN IMITATION OF Jesus Christ and simultaneously a martyrdom. It presents a no-less-forbidding appearance as a warfare and continuous struggle waged against the demon under the standard of Jesus Christ the King.

The ascetic life is a detachment, a separation from this world. Ascetic literature often viewed Israel's departure from Egypt as the prototype of departure from the world of sin, by means of ascesis. The Chosen People of Israel who left Egypt and sought to enter the Promised Land was still forced to continue an unremitting struggle against its enemies. Many of the Fathers took this as the starting point for their teaching that the ascetic, who also desires to leave the world, should be under no illusion that his pilgrimage will be calm and untroubled. He too will have to struggle, day after day, against the difficulties of the spiritual life, against his own passions, against the ambushes set for him by his enemies, and in particular by the demon, the enemy of all good.

St Nilus, a profound master of the spiritual life, had every reason to call the monk, and the ascetic in general, "a warrior who attacks the passions". In his Rule, St Benedict too speaks of battle as something essential to every kind of ascetic life. In his Prologue he says that every candidate for the monastic-ascetic life must be a soldier, ready to do battle for Jesus Christ, the true King, and must equip himself with the noble weapons of obedience. He calls the cenobite a "combatant" who fights under a Rule and an Abbot, while the hermit, in his opinion, has already learned to fight against the demon before withdrawing into the desert in order to attack him in single combat.

The idea of doing battle for Jesus Christ, in the way that we have portrayed it, is altogether scriptural.

It would be a fatal illusion to think that the Gospel's sole object and the aim of the religion taught by Jesus Christ, was to infiltrate and quietly transform the sphere of public and private life, without stirring up either crises or trouble. The reality of the Christian life is quite otherwise. The life of the Church is a continual struggle between two kingdoms: that of God and that of the Prince of this world. The same must be said of the work of sanctification in every individual. Let no one think that it should be seen as a slow, peaceful and orderly process of "divinization". Even the life of the simple faithful is characterized by continual struggle. Every part of our lives, every aspect of our being, one after another, must be torn from Satan's power. The idea of "warfare" is therefore fundamental for an understanding of the Christian life; it corrects the false idea that we often have — false because it is too abstract and comfortable — of the march towards holiness.

We are now between the first coming of Jesus Christ and his glorious return in the "last times" which precede the complete destruction of Satan's empire. Now he is making his "last push", his most terrible attack, so as to defend and perpetuate his reign. Is it not therefore logical that this struggle should make itself felt in a quite special way in the ascetic life, which is the most excellent form of Christian life?

* * *

St Benedict speaks of the ascetic who renounces self-will and takes up the weapons of obedience. This expression is obviously linked to the baptismal liturgy, which likewise speaks of renouncing Satan and all his pomps, his works. The word "pomp", as understood by the ancients, leads us to think of the soldier's life, as well as of religious life. Pomp meant the triumphal procession of the Prince of this world, which was precisely meant to demonstrate who were all those in his power. By baptism and the oath of faithfulness that the Christian makes to Christ, he separates himself from this procession, from this *taxis*, in order to join Jesus Christ's. And this is the definition of *apotaxis*, which means changing from fighting for one side to fighting for the other. It is a "detachment". It is also one of the most remarkable virtues in the ascetic sphere; it has in its very origins a military flavour and the scent of battle. The ascetic life cultivates detachment in a special way. Ascetics are

The Soldier of Jesus Christ

the picked troops of the army of Jesus Christ, troops who are so completely members of that army that they have completely broken with every aspect of civilian life, everything that belongs to the life of the ordinary citizen. By submitting to military discipline, the ascetic separates from the ordinary life of civilians; all his energies are devoted to carrying out the orders of his King, through a life of keeping rank and obeying.

The ascetic life — and this idea is also contained in the concept of *taxis* — the battle waged by the great army made up of the good angels and mankind. For these angels — and here we have in mind not a "multitude" of beings, but what we do indeed call an "army" — support the battle against the powers of darkness.

* * *

In one of his homilies, Origen speaks of two groups of spiritual soldiers; one does battle directly and is in contact with the enemy; while the other, in contrast, remains in the camp. The reason for this is that not everyone is capable of waging every kind of battle, in particular, doing battle with those who attack the word of God. Those capable of engaging such enemies are few in number, but their struggle is all the more glorious: "Fortunate are those who can do battle for all the people, defend God's people and carry off a rich booty."[1] The ascetic is already one of the special forces, but for all that, should not involve himself in just any battle, because there are struggles which require a special vocation, training and grace. Jesus Christ's army is an *acies ordinata*, an ordered battle line; each soldier awaits his orders and for his turn to come. Obedience clearly tells the ascetic when and how to do battle.

We can, however, get a clearer picture of the battlefield where every ascetic has to do battle with the enemy. The original meaning of *taxis* is the one which Sacred Scripture uses. St Luke speaks of "detachment", in the sense of leaving "the enemy's *taxis*". "Whoever of you does not renounce all, *apotassetai pasin* [*apotassetai pasin*], cannot be my disciple" (Lk. 14:33).

---

[1] Origen, *Hom. in Num.*, 25, 4: *Origène, Homélies sur les Nombres, III*, nouvelle édition par Louis Doutreleau, SJ (Sources chrétiennes [SC] 461, Cerf, Paris, 2001), p. 207.

According to Cassian, we are to distinguish three kinds of detachment: the *first*, which consists of contempt for all material things; the *second*, which separates us from all vices and every attachment to the fleshly life of the world; and the *third* which teaches us to scorn the things of this life and drive them completely from our souls; from then on, the soul concerns itself only with the contemplation of things invisible and eternal realities.[2] This description of the triple detachment simultaneously shows what elements make up the demon's *taxis* and what constitutes the *decorum* of the *pompa diaboli*. The ascetic strives for complete liberation, but given the fact that he cannot achieve this without effort, it is precisely in the triple detachment that his struggle and his combat will be found.[3]

All ascetic authors agree with Cassian on this fundamental affirmation: that the ascetic's struggle consists in the act of freeing himself from material things, from the passions and from earth-bound thoughts. Fortunate are those who, at the end of their lives, will be able to say that they have not only kept up the battle for the three-fold renunciation, but have also obtained the victory and have arrived at complete freedom of spirit.

Even so, this battle of the three-fold renunciation is not the hardest or highest of the struggles of the soldier of Christ. This is Origen's view:

> We have often said that Christians have a double struggle. The perfect and those who have got as far as St Paul and the Ephesians... battle against the evil spirits who dwell in the heavenly regions, while those less perfect and less advanced in spiritual life still struggle against flesh and blood.[4]

So there is a two-fold battle; the less perfect must work on the three-fold detachment, while the more perfect, on the other hand,

---

[2] Cassian, *On renunciations*, 3, 6, 1; John Cassian: The Conferences. Translated and annotated by Boniface Ramsey, O. P., Paulist Press, NY 1996 (ACW no. 57). p. 123

[3] The following chapter will show that the three degrees of detachment also correspond to the three principal stages of prayer.

[4] Origen, *Hom in Jesu Nave*, 11,4: *Origen: Homilies on Joshua*, translated by Barbara J. Bruce; FOTC vol. 105 (CUA Press, 2002), pp. 117–118.

do battle directly with the demon in person. Let us now briefly depict these two groups of combatants and set out their duties.

* * *

The ascetic's first battle is aimed at achieving freedom from material goods, and that is certainly no easy task. It is precisely because it is so difficult for us to separate ourselves from earthly things that are necessary for our needs that our Lord allowed his disciples two kinds of life. Some may remain in the world and, to a certain extent, enjoy it, while others will withdraw into the desert, or at any rate, into the company of ascetics, and so reduce to a minimum their contact with the world and the use of its goods. It is certainly not against the nature of Christian life to make use of the things of this world; a long list of saints shows that perfection can also be reached in the world. On the other hand, everyone knows that continuous involvement with the world and its affairs can easily hinder the free development of a more intense Christian life. That is why this abandonment of relations with the life of the world is a primary necessity for Christian ascetics, for monks and especially for hermits: "You love heavenly life," says St Basil to the one who comes to the monastery,

> you want to lead an angelic life and do battle in the company of Jesus Christ and his disciples. Very well! Then may you have the boldness to begin a difficult enterprise. Show yourself a man who is not held back by material ties.[5]

The monk must take care not to turn back to the things he has left behind. The danger of such a backsliding is real enough, for although there are many who, in a first generous and zealous impulse, leave goods, relations, worldly life, in order to become a monk, later comes the danger that, bit by bit, imperceptibly, they will reclaim what they left behind. The ascetic's commitment requires such detachment that he renounce all for God, from his first till his last moment. Speaking of St Benedict, St

---

[5] Basil, *Sermo de renuntiatione saeculi*, 2 (PG 31, 632): *Saint Basil: Ascetical Works*, On Renunciation of the World, translated by Sr. M. Monica Wagner, CSC; FOTC vol. 9 (CUA Press 1950), p. 18.

CHRISTIAN ASCETICISM

Gregory, explains this: "He had decided to give up all on this earth in order to regain it finally in heaven."[6] Such indeed is the ascetic's hope. He does not await a reward in this world, but in the next. There should be nothing material in the monastery to which the monk may attach his heart. The saints have always insisted on detachment, even to the extent of seeming uncompromising, if not unreasonable. We are given an example in the life of St Benedict: we are told that the saint threw out of the window a jar of oil which a monk, on the grounds that it was needed for the monastery, had refused to give to a poor man. That object, which remained available for the brethren as a result of the disordered attachment of a monk, seemed in the saint's eyes like something profaned, over which the demon's power had been exercised.

The Christian ascetic must break the closest and dearest ties. Like Jesus Christ on the cross, he must separate from all, even from his family and closest friends, in order to give himself solely to the one Master and submit himself to obedience. When the devil has not succeeded in blocking this generous action, he afterwards tries another way of twisting it. He tries to persuade the ascetic that this ideal which he formerly embraced with such dash, is false and illusory. He puts forward theories which advocate a certain "moderation". In such circumstances it is good to recall St Paul's saying, "An athlete is not crowned unless he competes according to the rules" (2Tim. 2:5). Because plenty of little reasons will soon appear for diluting the original zeal. St Basil goes as far as to say, "Don't think that all those who live in monks' cells will be saved.... Many embrace this way of life, but few really bear its yoke. The Kingdom of heaven is conquered by force and only the violent will take it" (Mt. 11:12).[7]

* * *

The force necessary to conquer the Kingdom of heaven is still more greatly needed in the second degree of detachment, the struggle against the passions of the soul.

---

6 *Dial.* II, 28
7 Basil, *Sermo de renuntiatione saeculi*, 2 (PG 31, 632) *On Renunciation of the World*, as above, (FOTC 9), p. 30

The Soldier of Jesus Christ

The Lord calls "force" the corporal mortification which the disciples of Jesus Christ choose freely. They renounce satisfying self-will and bodily rest in order to fulfil all Jesus Christ's commands. If you wish to seize the Kingdom of heaven, do violence to yourself and submit your body to the yoke of slavery. This yoke will bow down your head, but you can make it sweet and light by working to acquire the virtues, by fasting, vigils, obedience, manual work, by bearing all the insults that you will have to undergo from the demon and from men.[8]

St Basil, as a good psychologist and expert in the spiritual life, knows very well that the ascetic's burden is not lightened by dispensations and other mitigations. Only a committed struggle against softening, laziness and all the other fleshly tendencies can make Jesus Christ's yoke sweet and easy.

The second degree of detachment, the struggle against our natural inclinations, includes all that we usually sum up in the word "mortification". This is what mortification demands of the ascetic, this is the fundamental rule of Christian mortification.

In the monastic life, it is chiefly the Rule itself which performs this mortification. It is quite true that a Christian living in the world may perform harsher acts of mortification than a religious who does only what his Rule requires. Even so, regular life, taken over all, in itself represents a far from negligible mortification. Living day after day in accordance with a fixed and inflexible rule requires great steadfastness of will and great self-denial: silence, obedience, restrictions in sleep and all the rest presuppose continual renunciation. This regular life is not just intended as a rule to provide for a well-ordered life for the community; it is also intended as an exercise in continual mortification, and even as the primary mortification of religious. It seeks to help build the desire for detachment and separation from the world, to help in the war against the passions and to enrol volunteers in the ranks of Jesus Christ the King.

The struggle for the threefold detachment unfolds under the gaze of the angels, as the ancients observed. The hermit-ascetic,

---

8 *Ibid.*

perhaps hidden in a corner of the farthest desert, is never alone and left to his own devices. In the battle against the world and against his passions, he is taking his part in the great struggle between God's kingdom and Satan's empire. His is not a private struggle, but a battle supported by the whole Church, says Origen,

> by prayer, by fasting, by righteousness, by piety, by meekness, by chastity and all the virtues of continence. These are his weapons. If he returns to the camp victorious, then everyone, even the weak, those who were not called to the fight and were unable to go out to it, will rejoice at the afflictions and labours he has undergone.[9]

* * *

The second group of combatants is made up of those who struggle against Satan in person. If you talk about a direct, person-to-person struggle with the demon, you sometimes sense, especially nowadays, a sceptical reaction from your hearer. In every age, however, the lives of the saints tell us of this, and everyone knows what is related in the life of St Antony Abbot, the Great. In modern times, too, there have been saints who have had to struggle physically with the demon — it is enough to recall the Curé d'Ars, St John Vianney. The life of St Antony the Great clearly shows that open struggle with the demon is a sign of great holiness. We can see the same thing in the life of St Benedict. When the saint left Subiaco to found the monastery of Monte Cassino, "he had a change of scene, but not a change of enemy", as St Gregory comments.[10] And indeed the struggle became even fiercer, since the master of malice was attacking him undisguised.

The ascetic who has reached perfection, battling thus against the enemy, makes his way into his stronghold. Atop Monte Cassino, where St Benedict established his new dwelling-place, there already existed a temple of Apollo, evidence of Satan's

---

9   Origen, Hom. In Num., 25, 4, 1; *Origène, Homélies sur les Nombres*, III, nouvelle édition par Louis Doutreleau, SJ, Sources chrétiennes [SC] 461, Cerf, Paris, 2001, p. 205
10 *Dial.* II, 8, 10, p. 73

empire in that place. Besides this, there were groves nearby, dedicated to Apollo. The purifying and destructive activity of the saint could not do otherwise than infuriate the demon, who one day appeared before him in visible form to complain about being assaulted in this way. This is the same phenomenon as is related in the life of St Antony, when the saint withdrew into the desert to struggle personally against the principle of evil.

But the immediate struggle with the devil is waged in other ways besides hunting him down in his lair in the desert. Satan's reign is particularly visible in paganism and the infidel life. That is why St Benedict and many of his disciples have felt the need, whenever called to it by grace, to struggle against paganism by devoting themselves to the apostolate. They were certain that whoever has freed an immortal soul from the slavery of the devil may boast of having done battle with Satan on his home ground. Origen says as much of St Peter and St Paul, "They conquered and overcame all sorts of devils.... For indeed it is said that those who deliver people who are subject to demons, shed their own blood"[11]

* * *

The open struggle with the demons is clothed with profound significance. The ascetic who has attained the perfection of the first or the second detachment cannot be led into sin by external goods or his own passions. Even so, in this life there is no end to the struggle. Satan seeks victory to the very end, and refuses to relinquish his prey, and so he starts to show himself openly and to molest a man in every way. What are the chief weapons of the saints for this struggle? Above all, prayer. St Benedict's disciples called upon their Father, "to come and drive away the demon by means of his prayer."[12] Further, seeing the demon making a plaything of his brothers by making them see a non-existent fire in the kitchen, the holy patriarch, "bowed his head to pray."[13] Origen says the same, "By his prayer, a

---

11 Origen, Hom in Num., 25, 6, 3; *Origène, Homélies sur les Nombres*, III, nouvelle édition par Louis Doutreleau, SJ, Sources chrétiennes [SC] 461, Cerf, Paris, 2001, p. 217
12 *Dial.* II, 9, p. 75
13 *Dial.* II, 10, 2, p. 76

single saint is far stronger in the struggle than is a whole crowd of sinners."[14] Prayer unites the soul to God, and draws down God himself to earth. How, then, can the enemy resist? He has no choice but to withdraw. And this shows us a quite special aspect of Christian prayer. It is not a luxury, but something very serious and very laborious, because it is a struggle against the devil. That is why an old hermit said,

> I don't think there is anything harder than prayer. When a man wants to set himself to pray, that is when his enemies, the demons, try to prevent him. They know very well that nothing is more of an obstacle to their activities than prayer addressed to God. Every other good work, if you practise it perseveringly, leads to rest. Only prayer requires that you struggle to your last breath.[15]

We also need to see the prayer of the less-perfect Christian from the same point of view, because it, too, is a struggle against the demon. From that stems its value in the eyes of the Church, and the continual call that the Church makes on the prayer of its faithful.

If we have not yet reached perfect detachment, we are neither worthy nor capable of struggling openly against the demon. He is still using the simplest of means to stop us on the way of perfection. Since he still has a foothold in our souls, he can molest us through our passions. The life of the Church universal and victory in the great struggle between the kingdom of God and the kingdom of Satan requires real heroes. We still have and always must have great saints, perfect ascetics. Perhaps Satan would not have been able to extend his empire to such a fearful extent if they had been more numerous, struggling openly against him for the good of the people of God. However, the daily combat of all ascetics is already an effective battle against

---

14 Origen, Hom. In Num., 25, 2, 2; *Origène, Homélies sur les Nombres*, III, nouvelle édition par Louis Doutreleau, SJ, Sources chrétiennes [SC] 461, Cerf, Paris, 2001, p. 193
15 *Apophthegmata.* — "an old hermit". PG 65, 111C; *de abbate Agathone* 9 (18); Solesmes 91 Agathon

the enemy. The most hidden sacrifices and mortifications also have their significance and value, not just for the private good of the ascetic alone, but much more so in the great struggle for the kingdom of God. The serious practice of the ascetic life, whether that of the ascetic living in the world, or, more still, that of the hermit living hidden from the eyes of the world, is of great and universal importance. The idea of the ascetic life as struggle against the demon, characteristic of the ascetic who is a soldier of Christ, shows clearly the social importance of the ascetic life. This is the single combat of one soldier in Christ's great army, it is a part, but an important part, of the Church's perpetual struggle for the definitive triumph of God's kingdom.

CHAPTER 6
Silence

SEPARATION FROM THE WORLD AND growing union with God are shown exteriorly by the observance of silence. The world is full of disorder and tumult, while God gives peace and tranquillity: *tranquillus Deus tranquillat omnia*, the peaceful God pacifies everything, as St Bernard said. Silence has an extraordinary importance for progress in the spiritual life; without control of the tongue, one will never arrive at perfection. One day a monk said to a hermit, "What must I do about my tongue, which I cannot control?" The hermit replied, "When you speak, do you find rest?" The other was forced to admit that he did not, and so the hermit said, "If you do not find rest, then why do you speak?"[1]

The power of speech is unique to humans. It is a consequence of being rational, and distinguishes men from every other being, even angels. These can indeed communicate among themselves, but to call this language is a figurative use of the term.

Further, speech is part of the "supernatural" dignity of humanity, of being made in the image of God. God speaks, and thus sends forth the Word; a human, speaking a word, and so manifesting a thought, in some degree imitates God the Father, who manifests himself in the Word, his Son. This is the root of the human power of speech.

Further, whether considered from a natural or a supernatural viewpoint, the power of speech is such a privilege that we always and everywhere find rules intended to restrain its use as much as possible. Five centuries before Jesus Christ, Lao-Tse was already saying, "Whoever knows Lao, does not speak; whoever speaks, does not know him". Silence in the mystery religions is famous, it forbade initiates to speak about religious matters to those who would not understand them. Others said, God is so ineffable that human speech cannot speak adequately of him; it

---

[1] *Apophthegmata* PG 65, 307B; de abbate Nisteroo 3; Solesmes 558, Nisteros 3

is rather by silence that mankind venerates him, showing in that way that he has understood his greatness, which goes beyond every human concept.

Certain non-Christian mystics and philosophers gave thought to God's own silence. God is constantly at work in nature, sustains everything, nourishes everything, but does so without any noise; no voice is heard, not a mutter amid all that work; man, too, if he wishes to be perfect and like to God, should not utter many words, that will not make him heard.

The Christian idea of silence takes up some of these concepts and gives them deeper meaning, based on a clearer doctrine of the value both of the word and of silence.

We have already alluded to the idea that the human word is in some sense an imitation of the intra-Trinitarian procession, the generation of the Word. Man is thus a true image of God, not when he encloses himself in silence, but when he utters a good and holy word, the only kind which can reflect the divine Word.

There we already see the first and fundamental difference between the non-Christian and the Christian concept. The difference consists of that effect of sin, which according to revealed teaching, broke the harmony between man and God. Sin brought it about that man's word is no longer in conformity with God's Word, and so the image of God is darkened and corrupted.

St Ambrose was entirely correct in reducing the first sin to misuse of speech. Man should have conformed to God's Word; when he uttered a word, he was not independent, but instead obliged to take the divine word as his rule. Connecting this idea with the fact that in the Old Testament God demanded of his people a constant attention to what he was revealing to them, the saint goes on, "Eve fell as a result of her saying to her husband what she had not heard from God, her Lord. The first word of God says to you, 'Listen'."[2] From the moment of the first fault, human speech was no longer what it should have been,

---

2 Ambrose, *De officiis*, 1, 2, 7. *On the Duties of the Clergy: Select Works and Letters*, translated by E. Romestin, Nicene and Post-Nicene Fathers of the Christian Church, 2nd Series, Vol. X (T&T Clark, Edinburgh, Wm. B. Eerdmans, reprint March 1989), p. 2.

it was no longer the faithful image of the Word, consubstantial with God. Much more, since the first sin was related to a disorder in human speech, which had sought its guiding principle not in God, but in the serpent's seductive word, that same human speech would henceforward express disobedience to God and the disorder which had come about in the depths of the soul. So it is no surprise that after this first fault, God should rightly have punished the whole of humanity by means of this faculty of speech by withdrawing the extraordinary grace that having a single shared language represented, the surest guarantee of unity among the human race. The confusion of tongues following the building of the Tower of Babel begins the long series of humanity's divisions, into races, peoples, languages, and their fruit in wars, quarrels, misunderstandings that will go on until the complete re-establishment of God's kingdom. After the first sin and its disastrous consequences, whoever keeps silence may consider themselves as having the right relationship to God. Man has fallen from the heavenly places of Paradise, where he could converse familiarly with God to those dark regions which separate him from his Creator. His very language shows him how God has become naturally inaccessible to his nature: human words, bound to purely natural means and incomparably inferior, cannot adequately express the divine transcendence. Still today, even though by the work of Jesus Christ sin has been abolished, and though, in some sense, a direct and familiar conversation of man with God has been restored to him (and the mystical state is precisely that), human words cannot find words to express that experience.

This is precisely what St Paul says about his ecstasy, when he was snatched up to Paradise and heard ineffable words which it was not permitted (he means "possible") for a man to speak (2 Cor. 12:4).

This truth is expressed still more clearly in the fourth century apocryphal gospel of Nicodemus. Two witnesses of Jesus Christ's descent to hell, who have come back to life on the day of the Redeemer's death, tell their friends living on the earth a part of what they have seen. However, they cannot tell them everything:

We are not allowed to speak of the other mysteries of God. The Archangel Michael told us, "Go to Jerusalem to your brothers to pray aloud and glorify the resurrection of the Lord Jesus Christ, who has raised you with Him. However, do not speak to anyone, remain seated and speechless until the Lord Himself at the appropriate time allows you to tell of his mysteries."[3]

So, according to the Christian understanding, man, burdened with sin and not yet entirely set free, is subject to the limitations of his fragile human nature, not yet glorified. Since he cannot ever express the mysteries of God as they deserve, his task is to adore God in reverent silence.

St Benedict sums up this idea in a single sentence of his Rule, when he says, "It is for the master to speak and teach, it is fitting for the disciple to be silent and listen."[4] The master is God, who speaks through the mouth of the Abbot, while the monk's attitude is that of the disciple, who listens.

Everything that has resulted from sin must go. The tumult of empty words, evil thoughts, disordered desires must be silent for ever. The sound of the Redemption has echoed through the region of death, and so, through the region of silence. The whole process of mortification and purification to which the ascetic submits, is impossible without silence. Speech, desires, even thoughts — or at any rate, those which go against God and prevent the rebirth of the new man — must be silenced.

* * *

But God did not wish that man should remain forever mute. In his creation he himself gave him the wonderful power of being able to express his thoughts, and so enter into spiritual contact with others, and then in the Redemption he to repair and put right his creation. He therefore sent his divine Word, so that in him mankind could rediscover his true speech and direct it to God.

---

3 *Apocryphal Gospel of Nicodemus*, 2nd part, ch. 2; *The Apocryphal New Testament, Being the Apocryphal Gospels, Acts Epistles, and Apocalypses*, newly translated by Montague Rhodes James, (Oxford, Clarendon Press, 1924), p. 117 ff.

4 RB 6:6

Silence

So Christian asceticism doesn't mean that kind of quietism that sees perfection as consisting simply and solely in a triple silence — silence from every word, from every aspiration and every thought. It is quite true that the Christian ascetic tends to regulate speech by avoiding excess of evil words. The Christian ascetic also mortifies the desires of the flesh and vain thoughts, but differs from the quietist in not seeing the ideal as a purely negative standpoint; the Christian ascetic does not hope to arrive at the "mystic silence" of union with God by mortification alone, and by the simple fact of keeping silence. In its very principle, the Christian ascetic's task has a positive direction; it is nourished by holy thoughts and desires, it listens to holy words, it only reduces to silence whatever is vicious.

Protected by silence, the germ of divine life grows in the soul. This germ is participation in the divine Word, which will make man like to the only Son of God in all things. St Ambrose warns us, "Our mouth is a door which we should only open to admit Jesus Christ.... What have you to do with other? Speak with Jesus Christ alone. Let Jesus Christ be your only companion in speech."[5] Many authors sum up the whole of mystical experience in these words or others like them: one will often repent of having spoken, but never of having kept silent. Tranquillity of soul makes it more capable of hearing the divine voice.

The divine Word, our soul's guest, leads us to know the "Father from whom he proceeds, not by a simple outpouring, but truly to lead us back to him. Our sharing in the divine Word is thus simultaneously the beginning of our return to the Father. The word expressed in prayer shows this clearly. Prayer is our response, the echo to God's voice in our soul, our first meeting with the heavenly Father. Our natural powers are insufficient to express such a word. "The spirit comes to the help of our weakness, because we do not know what we ought to ask, according to our needs in our prayers. But the Spirit himself prays for us through inexpressible groanings" (Rom. 8:26).

In prayer, man rediscovers his voice. The Acts of the martyrdom of St Polycarp tell us how the venerable bishop, at the

---

[5] Ambrose *De virginitate*, c. 13; PL. 16, c. 300, 233 (80) C

moment of being captured by his persecutors, asked permission to pray. "He prayed, and for two whole hours he prayed and could not stop, filled as he was with divine grace, so that everyone who was there was filled with a holy awe." In his letter to the Romans, speaking of the Holy Spirit, St Ignatius of Antioch expresses himself thus: "The living water (the Holy Spirit) is living in me; this water speaks within me, and says to me, 'Come to the Father'." St Ambrose expresses the same thought, when he explains why the priest Zachary remained dumb:

In this one man, the whole people became dumb.... Sacrifices ended, the prophets became mute; all this is expressed in the silence of the prophet and in the silence of the priest (Zachary).... For God, in taking away the Word which he had been accustomed to communicate to the Prophets took away from them the prophets themselves. For us, however, the Word of God has come down to us, and is not silent.[6]

The fact of our sanctification and our participation in the divine Word demand that the ascetic not remain silent forever, but that from silence he pass to holy speech, to prayer. In its most perfect state that can once more return to silence, at least externally, since by this stage the human voice is no longer capable of expressing the depth of the soul's intimate union with God.

So, in the life of the ascetic, silence signifies the necessary passage from the tumult of this world of sin to the purity of the holy spheres where God dwells. Through progressive sanctification, he rediscovers the power of being able to direct his speech towards God in prayer. And even, after a long and serious life of ascesis, spent in silence and prayer, and by a special impulse of divine grace, he may in this way rediscover the power of communicating the Word of God to men, as a spiritual master or as an Apostle. Then the saying which the Pentecost liturgy applies to the Apostles will be true of him: "They were all filled with the Holy Spirit and began to speak."

---

6 Ambrose, *In Luc.*, I, 40: *Commentary of Saint Ambrose on the Gospel according to Saint Luke*, trans. Íde M. Ní Riain M. A., B. Phil Saint Andrews (Elo Publications, Dublin), 2001; p. 22

CHAPTER 7

The Life of Prayer

CHRISTIAN ASCETICISM REQUIRES prayer. The ascetic is a pilgrim who distances himself from this world to follow Christ. But Jesus, "In the morning, while it was still very dark, got up and went out to a deserted place, and there he prayed" (Mk. 1:35). In his turn, the ascetic leaves the world and withdraws, like Christ, into a desert place, not only with the object of separating himself from the world, but, more importantly, to enter a higher and holier world of union with God. Leaving the world of sin and entering the world of God are two sides of the same coin. This union with God is brought about by the life of prayer, founded on the sacraments and the liturgy, and private prayer is simply its continuation. The close links between the ascetic life (departure from this world of sin) and the life of prayer (entry into the world of God) find expression, one might say, in the very order of the chapters of St Benedict's Rule: first the holy lawgiver sets out the ascetic teaching on obedience, silence and humility, then come the chapters on prayer, which are the crown and fruit of the ascetic life. Separation from the world and progress in prayer are not two separate stages, two degrees, but rather two different aspects of the one reality, our progress in holiness. Abandoning this world and making progress in prayer are closely connected realities. The very names given to the various states of prayer show this: there is a very high state of prayer known as "ecstasy", of which the exact meaning is being outside the body, outside the natural, outside the world. So if we want to explain how the soul can "leave this world", prayer supplies the explanation, but for that we need to be able to show how the soul's ascent through the various degrees of prayer simply corresponds to deeper entry into the world of God.

St Nilus expresses the relationship between the ascetic life and the life of prayer like this, "Sell what you have and give it to the poor; take up the cross, renounce yourself, and you will be able to pray without distraction."[1]

The early Church was more insistent about bodily attitude for prayer than the Church is nowadays. Liturgical prayers were recited with extended arms and facing the east, because it was believed that Christ had departed from the world in that direction and would also return from the same direction. The arms extended towards the east expressed the desire to follow Jesus Christ and to leave the world with him. St Thomas expressed a preference for prayer facing East, "because Christ, the light of the world, is also called *Oriens*, the rising star, and it is said of him that 'he went up above the heavens eastwards'".[2]

If one views the ascetic life as a departure from this world and an imitation of Christ, it becomes clear how essential to it is the life of prayer. The two concepts — leaving the world and imitation of Christ — need prayer as their positive complement. If one thought that the ascetic life and imitation of Christ were merely negative, consisting of mortification, detachment and all that is toilsome, that would be a misunderstanding.

* * *

If we view the ascetic life in the way just suggested, it is immediately obvious that prayer, on the same basis as detachment from the world and imitation of Christ, is something strictly supernatural. The same Holy Spirit is at work in the holy martyrs and the great monks and shows himself to the soul possessing the gift of prayer. Prayer's supernatural character is very important. Yes, prayer would have been possible, even in a state of pure nature, and without being raised to share in the intimate life of God, but the prayer of a man in that state would have been very different from ours. In a state of pure nature, man could indeed have praised and thanked his Creator, and set before God's mercy his needs and poverty. All

---

[1] Nilus, *On Prayer* 17 (PG 79, 1171A)
[2] Aquinas, *Summ. theol.*, IIa IIae, q. 183, a 3 ad 3: *Vol. 47, The Pastoral and Religious Lives (2a2ae. 183–9)*. Latin Text, English Trans., introduction and Glossary by Jordan Aumann O. P. (Chicago, Illinois. Blackfriars 1973), p. 11

the same, historically speaking, that state of pure nature never existed, since Adam was, from the very beginning, created by God in a state of grace. This state of original justice was then destroyed by the sin of our first parents, and as a result of that sin, mankind no longer remained on good terms with God, but found himself in a state of enmity, turned away from God, a situation which only the grace of baptism could remedy. To have relations with his Creator on the same high level as Adam had in the earthly Paradise, was not possible for man before being set at rights with God in this way. That is why the unreasoning part of creation itself, which for Adam was a mirror in which he could contemplate his Creator, now underwent a certain devilish influence, as a result of which, instead of leading him to the Creator, it very often detaches us from him, and leads man to admire or even adore the beauty of nature, often becoming enslaved to it. If man stops at admiration for nature itself, he has only gone half-way, not realising that it is God's instrument for drawing man to Him. Most unfortunately, this is the attitude that men very often take today, turning their back on God. Contrariwise, for the holy man, unreasoning nature is itself one of the most effective ways of turning him to God, as we see in an extraordinary way in the case of St Francis of Assisi.

Man separated from God cannot make proper use of unreasoning creation, that is to say, as a way to find God; without the help of grace, he cannot pray. With the Apostles, he too must turn to Jesus and ask him, Lord, teach us to pray. Jesus taught us to pray when he was on earth to carry out his work of redemption. Prayer then, or at any rate the kind of prayer that God wants of us, is not something that springs up spontaneously from our hearts, it comes from Jesus Christ Himself. Like our return to God, prayer has its objective norms.

That Christian prayer has its rules and has an objective norm is not perhaps something to which we give sufficient attention; and when we say that prayer has its rules, we are talking chiefly about what people call private, personal prayer, rather than exclusively of liturgical prayer. All the ancient authors say that we should follow our Lord's example, and not begin our private prayer with requests. Rather, we should begin by praising God, and then go on to an act of compunction, struck by the contrast between the greatness of the divine majesty whom we adore and our littleness; realizing our nothingness and boldness. From compunction we go on to acts of thanksgiving for all the gifts given to the Church, for all those we have personally received, both in the order of nature and in the order of grace. Only then should we put our requests, both for the Church's present needs and for our own.

* * *

The author of the monastic Constitutions attributed to St Basil says, "When you apply yourself to prayer, detach yourself from yourself, from your wife, from your children. Leave the earth, rise up above the heavens, free yourself from visible and invisible creatures, and begin by glorifying the Creator of the universe." Prayer, then, presupposes detachment, it requires separation from the world. For man standing alone before God, adoration and glorification follow of themselves, almost naturally. The same author goes on, "Therefore begin by saying humbly, 'Truly, Lord, I am a great sinner, unworthy to speak to you.'" That is the second task in Christian prayer, to accuse oneself of one's sins. Thanksgiving follows, "I thank you Lord, for having patiently put up with my sins, and for not having punished me for them before now." Our author goes on with his teaching, "Only then, ask what you have to ask, but not so much in the way of material goods as in matters related to the Kingdom of God, as he has laid upon you." In order to encourage us, he ends like this,

> And if you ask things worthy of God, do not give up asking until you have received them.... And if a month passes, or a year, or three or four years, or even longer, without your receiving an answer, don't relax your prayer." God never fails in his promises, and Holy Writ supplies noteworthy examples. They show that God never abandons those who pray trustingly and perseveringly.

This instruction is not unique of its kind, for Origen, too, at the end of his treatise on prayer, teaches in exactly the same way how to pray in a truly Christian way.

* * *

Christian prayer is therefore the positive aspect of our detachment from the world of sin, and since it is the way into the world of the divine it has a dynamic character. As it progresses in detachment from earthly things, the soul has constantly to perfect itself more and more, it cannot sit still, but must grow and climb until it reaches the highest degree of union with God. The ascetic who makes progress in mortification and in the spiritual life in general does not always pray in the same way, and just as a certain amount of progress in the ascetic life is necessary, so in some sense does progress in prayer become mandatory.

We all know that there are different degrees in prayer; all the masters of prayer say so. These degrees are always part of an ascending scale directed towards perfect union. We shouldn't assume that these are reserved for a small number of "specialists" and a luxury of the spiritual life — quite the contrary, these degrees are the ladder to paradise that all want to and must climb. We all are to pass through these degrees of prayer, we all must reach the summit, if we are to reach perfect union with God. If we do not reach it in this life, then before we enter paradise we will have to pass through the painful purification of purgatory.

So progress in prayer is a serious matter. It is serious, and it is not easy, because it simultaneously involves separation from the world. You leap heavenwards by leaving the earth behind. That is why the saints often accompany their prayers with harsh ascetical practices. That is why prayer is one of the most effective means for battling the devil, who tries by every possible means to prevent our ascent and tie us to the earth. The heavenly ladder, both of prayer and of humility, are one and the same thing, expressed in three different ways. On cannot climb the ladder to paradise while remaining on the bottom rung of the ladder of humility. Rightly does St Benedict conclude the seventh chapter of his Rule, on humility, with the mystical state: "Having thus climbed all the degrees of humility, the monk will quickly arrive at the perfect love of God, which drives out fear." Perfect charity is pure prayer, mystical prayer. Other masters of Christian antiquity say the same. For Cassian, for example, charity and contemplation are indistinguishable, but make one single perfection, in that perfect charity is only to be found in contemplation alone, and vice versa.

* * *

Prayer, then, is inseparable from the ascetic life. Whoever leaves the world approaches God, praying.

St Benedict's life is a good illustration of this. Every aspect of his life is accompanied by prayer. In every need, he has recourse to prayer. In order to obtain for his brothers the water they needed, tells St Gregory, his biographer, "he clambered up the rocks, accompanied by little Placid, and prayed for a long time."[3] On another occasion, says St Gregory, "the brothers were outside, putting up a wall, and the man of God remained in his cell, praying."[4] Some pilgrims climbed Monte Cassino, "to commend themselves to the intercession of the servant of God".[5] At the end of the Life, so as to convey an idea of the great holiness of the Patriarch, St Gregory the Great tells of the famous vision of St Benedict. The life of this saint was truly a life of prayer. Desiring to progress in the life of prayer is not to desire something reserved for a small number of mystical souls, but simply to desire perfection. An ascetic who made no effort to progress in the life of prayer would not make any progress in any direction. He would not detach himself from the world, nor would he approach God.

* * *

If one wants to have a more solid grasp of what constitutes progress in the life of prayer, and how it comes about in the soul of the Christian ascetic, then the starting-point needs to

---

3 *Dial.* II, 5:2, p. 68
4 *Ibid.*, 11:1, p. 76
5 *Ibid.*, 13:1, p. 77

be that such progress is part of our imitation of Jesus Christ and of the return to the Father.

Man's return to the Heavenly Father only really happens after death, but even so, progress in the life of prayer is already something of an anticipation of it during our mortal life. The old definition of prayer here gains a much more concrete meaning: it is a raising of the soul to God, not merely a raising of thought, but of the whole soul.

Our true return to the Father, which comes later and is both an imitation and a consequence of the Ascension of Jesus to Heaven, is distinguished from Christ's in two essential points. Jesus Christ ascended to Heaven by his own power, whereas man must be carried aloft by angels, by supernatural powers. The life of St Benedict tells that when that venerable Father "concentrated his attention on that ray of brilliant light, he saw the soul of Germanus, Bishop of Capua, carried to heaven by angels in a fiery globe"[6]. The ancients were very familiar with the teaching that the human soul arrived in heaven, led by angels who entrusted it to St Michael, "Provost of Heaven" (*praepositus paradisi*). Man cannot, by his own strength alone, raise himself as high as God, to return to Him by entering paradise.

Our ascension, besides, takes place gradually, that is a second difference, and one should not imagine our ascension as a continuous upward movement. That is a very important point. When the ancients spoke about it, they never left out its various stages, and their teaching is very useful to us in explaining the soul's ascension in prayer. Many writers of Christian antiquity state that the soul, when it leaves this world, must pass through the different dwellings of the demons in the air. The demons examine the soul to discover whether or not it has something about it which belongs to them, vices or imperfections, for until it has been purified of all this dross, it is unable to continue on its journey. While it is being purified, the soul is also instructed in matters divine by the good angels, so that it will be able to understand the mysteries of God and be more worthy of appearing before his throne. This series of purifications and

---

[6] *Ibid.*, 35:3, p. 105

instructions goes on as long as is necessary for the soul to be completely purified and to reach the fullness of understanding.

It is not our purpose to discuss here the truth of this scheme of purification and post-mortem progress in perfection; it is not generally accepted in all its details nowadays. All the same, it has also been applied to that anticipation of our ascension brought about in the life of prayer, and in that case, the teaching which we have just been setting out, expresses absolutely undeniable truths.

All writers on the spiritual life agree that perfection can only be acquired by constant ascetic battle and by assiduous meditation on eternal truths; in that way the soul is freed from its worldly attachments and sees the true value of the things that last for eternity. Several authors say that the soul which desires to be purified so as to attain union with God must pass through three stages; it must first of all reach an accurate estimation of the external world, and in the light of that, of itself. Once it has achieved this double clarification, the soul moves on without more ado to the third stage, contemplation of and union with God.

* * *

The knowledge and contemplation of external things being spoken of here is not something philosophical, still less something technical. These two modes of knowledge of the material world, despite their importance and undeniable usefulness for man remain, even so, imperfect and inferior. It is quite clear that philosophical knowledge can never inform us about the ultimate reason for material creation, give us the answer as to why it was created—only revelation can do that. Apart from its imperfection, technical knowledge, on the other hand, contains a danger. Certainly God had endowed man with the power to rule the world of non-rational creatures and to make use of them for his purposes. Furthermore, this represents an element of re-conquest of that mastery over external things which Adam had received as a special grace in the earthly paradise. The imbalance which sin brought into the world often results, instead of man's mastery over creatures, in a reversal of this: more often than not man is no longer master of the created; it is things, machines, all today's institutions and discoveries, which master and subject man to a shameful enslavement. Day after day, modern life proves the truth of this.

Instead, this knowledge of external things which is necessary to the spiritual life and to prayer, precisely consists of the recognition of Satan's empire, of being aware of how much power he has over the visible world, of understanding the true place which material things should have in God's plan and in the work of the redemption of humanity.

Such knowledge cannot remain confined to the realm of theory, the soul must simultaneously put it into practice, by freeing itself from every disordered attachment to creatures which is incompatible with a life of union with God. This teaching, the soul must receive from the angels, and does so in fact, since no purely natural science and no human science could supply it. Such is the campaign which the soul must wage against the demons trying to block or hinder its ascension heavenwards. Since this is a long-term effort, this teaching and this campaign represent the first "dwelling" in which the soul which is detaching itself from the world in order to go to God, must take up residence.

After the apprenticeship and the struggle of the first stage, the soul comes to the second stage. It passes from the external world to the internal world, to its own heart, with all its merits and failings. This is where the second stage takes place. Instruction carries on, in order to learn the true value of the soul, and the battle intensifies, because now it engages with and must bring under control the injurious affections and inclinations of the heart itself. The soul must learn to know itself, to see itself as God sees it, it must convince itself of its own nothingness, free itself from its egotism and the mistaken opinion which it has of itself—in other words, it must get rid of its self-will. This last renunciation is the most difficult, and cannot be achieved except at the cost of ruthless and unremitting struggles and mortifications.

Once this stage has been passed, union with God and contemplation are the automatic result. The soul is henceforth free of all attachment to anything which is not God.

So, ascent in the life of prayer and contemplation must therefore simultaneously be an ascetic climb. By contemplation the soul frees itself from creatures and from all that is not of God, it purifies itself. It is clear that such a purification takes place by degrees and that the ascent does not follow an unvarying rhythm. It is indeed accompanied by constant ascetic effort and by constant practice of detachment and abnegation. Our nature is so rooted in disordered love that a single meditation or a single act of renunciation are not enough to set it free. It is not enough to meditate from time to time on material things, on the external world and on oneself; during these meditations, the soul must stop for a while and dwell on these thoughts, make them the constant object of its prayer, and, at the same time, battle with noxious attachments and our natural inclination towards sin.

If these meditations are to be profitable for the interior life, the ascetic should not be in too much of a hurry over them. No real progress can result from meditations and ascetic exercises made sporadically or too hastily. Even if it is embraced with a certain generous impulse, the ascetic life cannot lead to perfection if work and other occupations are so many as to leave insufficient time for assiduous practice of the necessary exercises. Work alone does not lead to holiness.

Another danger can completely shackle the effect of these meditations, or at any rate greatly reduce their effect; this is the danger of not setting them in concrete reality. Meditating in the abstract on the value of external realities is not enough, the ascetic must examine himself concretely on those material things with which he is in constant contact, he must consider his attachments to his own family, to his country, his interest in current affairs; he must assess his strengths, gifts and limitations and seek to free himself from every attachment and every vanity. All the beautiful meditations in the world on the mysteries of the faith and the life of the Lord cannot, of themselves, cause the soul to climb the ladder to paradise. If they are made well, these meditations can help to strengthen, to invigorate; they can nourish and console, but the essential, especially at the beginning of the climb, is to look to oneself, to consider one's

The Life of Prayer

state, to examine our relationship with the world, as well as our relationship with God.

An ascetic who goes on in meditation, in prayer and in ascetical exercises in this way will certainly reach a state of great peace, of rest for the soul. He will experience contemplative rest (*quies contemplationis*), as opposed to the "tumult" of worldly distraction. Whoever judges the exterior world at its true value and has a low esteem for himself is no longer the plaything of his surroundings, nor of his passions and vain desires, but is able to enjoy peace of soul. Every ascetic who seriously practises this degree of contemplative live will attain to this. That is why this first degree of more perfect prayer, this first stage on the way to heaven, is called by a name which emphasizes its positive side: "the prayer of quiet".

The prayer of quiet necessarily leads to a still higher state. A man who is freed from external things and disordered attachments is thereby set "outside the world" of sin, and once he has been freed from his self-will, he is also "outside himself". There is something here of "ecstasy", properly so-called, since as the word suggests, it means precisely, to be outside oneself.

The prayer of quiet, when it reaches perfection, leads to "ecstatic prayer", in which the ascetic is no longer distracted by anything, and so can concentrate on the vision of God, on delight in invisible and heavenly things.

In its final stage of perfection, ecstatic prayer becomes "transforming union", in which prayer man dwells only on God, eternal mysteries, Jesus Christ, and the glory of the saints; conversing with God himself, he loses all contact with this world below and is gradually transformed interiorly. He comes to take on the nature of the things he constantly contemplates in prayer; uninterrupted converse with God causes him to share further in the divine nature.

These three degrees of the life of prayer, which we meet in one form or another in all ascetic authors, supply theological meaning to the ancient teaching on the ascent of the soul to heaven, applied to the interior life. The road which every ascetic must follow in order to reach perfection is accompanied by progress in prayer, as we have described it.

It is true that other authors offer a description of the degrees of prayer which at first sight seems a bit different from this. Prayer of quiet, for instance, is called "prayer of imperfect union", and in it the soul experiences the presence of God, but distractions remain possible. In this scheme, the second degree is "prayer of perfect union", which does not allow any distraction. Union with God can reach such an intensity that even the activity of the senses completely ceases. The soul can no longer interrupt prayer, because it is completely governed and led by God's action. The last and highest degree is transforming union, also called mystical marriage. The union of the soul with God has become constant, and not even external material activities interrupt it any more.

This difference in the way the degrees of prayer are taught and described is merely accidental. The description we have given, unlike the alternative description, does not take as its starting point what one might call a psychological viewpoint (the presence or absence of distractions, etc.,) but an ontological one: man freed from disordered attachments finds rest; having left the world and left himself, he is transformed into God. The two viewpoints do not exclude one another, but are mutually complementary. The threefold progress in the life of prayer — and this clearly emerges from what we have been saying so far — is not the preserve of a few mystical souls, but an advance which is necessary and indispensable for anyone who wishes to lead an ascetic life.

The life of prayer and the ascetic life are complementary. The things of this world lose their worth for the ascetic in exact proportion to his advance in knowledge of God and contemplation. He will experience for himself what St Gregory the Great said of St Benedict's great vision, "For a soul which sees the Creator, all created things seem small, because even that little which the soul can see of the light of the Creator, is enough to reduce every created thing to something small."[7] Lifted up out of this world by God's grace, the ascetic enters a new world, becoming a citizen of the city of God and sharing the angelic life through

---

7 *Dial.*, 35:6, p. 106

contemplation. Abba Macarius used to say of a monk whom he always found absorbed in deep prayer every time he went to visit him, "He is an angel on this earth." That is indeed a good description of the ascetic who has passed through the three stages of which we have spoken.

* * *

It would however be mistaken to have the impression that the ascetic, even if he has reached a high degree of perfection, can live in uninterrupted contemplation, in "vision" of God. Such a favour, far from being granted to all, is a rare gift and a personal privilege. Nonetheless, a living experience of their union with God is open to all, at least at certain moments. And it is not possible that any ascetic worthy of the name should not from time to time really become aware of the greatness of God and the insignificance of the created world. Moments like these are the happiest for disciples of Jesus Christ who are vowed to the search for God, moments in which they taste the fruit of their painful ascetic labour, they experience God, they "see" him. For a few moments they return to the happiness that was Adam's in the earthly paradise. Adam always lived in the "peace of silence", as St Gregory the Great puts it. Without suffering, without a struggle, without having to pass through the narrow door of the threefold detachment, he possessed peace of soul. Adam was not a soldier as we are, he had no need to conquer peace, he already possessed it, as a free gift from the Creator. His heart and soul were always busy with God.

Sin caused the loss of these good things, and man fell "below himself," because he gave himself up to creatures, and he lost the "vision" of God; he lost sight of God. Blindness replaced that vision of delight. God was lost, so it was necessary to go in search of him and of peace, for interior silence had given way to battle within. Man had "fallen below himself", to use St Gregory the Great's expression, by which he means that flesh and spirit struggle together, that man is more inclined to fleshly than to spiritual thoughts; that henceforth man will not contemplate God in direct experience of the Creator's presence, as beforehand, but will only do so in the very imperfect mirror of material creation. That also means that love for passing things has been substituted for the love of God, and that in the depths of the soul peace and tranquillity no longer reign, but only the constant rumour of distractions and the riot of vain and useless thoughts.

The ascetic frees himself from that state with the help of grace. The exercise of constant meditation, together with detachment, becomes a positive "tomb", to borrow another of St Gregory's expressions, in which man hides himself and mystically dies to the world, to his earthly leanings and finally to himself. Use of the word "tomb", when applied to meditation, gives a special emphasis to the fact that the ladder of mortification is identical to the ladder of contemplation. The tomb and death parallel Resurrection and new life; the ascetic rises "above himself" in the rest which he used to enjoy in the earthly paradise by the gift of God's grace. He returns to the region of silence and rest in God. *Mutabilia cuncta transcendens, ipsa iam in tranquillitate quietis suae, in mundo extra mundum est,* says St Gregory, that man who is still living in the world is already outside the world in the tranquillity of his rest, the result of his renunciation of passing things. The man devoted to contemplation frees himself from the world and its laws, and fleshly concupiscence no longer provides the motivation for his actions. St Gregory the Great illustrates this state by the example of Job. His friends, even his wife, accuse and calumniate the holy man, but these are blows which fall "beneath him"; "above himself", his spirit contemplates God and is fixed on him. St Gregory the Great calls this state of the contemplative soul "rapture", but he is certainly not using it in the same sense as modern mystics. They speak of rapture as a kind of ecstasy, whereas St Gregory's primary purpose is to express the fact that, of himself, man does not have the strength to reach contemplation, and therefore needs to be carried up to it by a higher power, lifted up to it by divine power. This help from God does violence, one could say, insofar as it runs contrary to the inclinations of the flesh and fallen nature, and this is why he calls it "rapture".

By advancing in contemplation, the most intimate depth of the human soul undergoes transformation, it expands; the

The Life of Prayer

divine light brings about this enlargement. The light of contemplation gives the soul a power that is almost divine, now it sees things that it could not see beforehand, *videre sine difficultate potuit omne, quod infra Deum est*, it can without difficulty see everything, because it is less than God. The depth of the soul in which the most secret actions of the soul take place (St Gregory calls it the *sinus animae*) is submitted to the action of divine grace. Its powers increase, its blindness to the things of God disappears, the human heart is no longer closed in on itself by the egotistical self-interest of fallen nature; instead it enlarges, opens up to make room for what it had never tasted before, for what it did not know. As we said, in Adam, contemplation was a "state". Locked into that union with God, he resembled Him who "holds himself" unmoved when all else passes and falls back into nothingness. As for us, held back by sin, we need to rise up again in order to see the divine light. Again according to St Gregory, this rising again and this lifting up take place through "rapture", *raptim*. So the moments granted us to enjoy contemplation are relatively brief. The "stability" of Adam's perfection is not given back to us then. We must always be renewing our striving, our search, to receive afterwards the reward of a few moments of consolation and real joy, a short foretaste of the beatitude to come, *tenuiter et latenter*, lasting and enduring. We see the light of dawn for a few short seconds, but are not yet bathed in its light. That is how God shows himself to those who seek the face of the Lord, the rays of divine light briefly illuminate the darkness in which our way is wrapped. Adam dwelt continually in that light, and we must try to make our way to that light, even though few attain it in this life, and that only for a brief while, after which they fall back into blind darkness.

God is light. Being illuminated by the divine light is, therefore, to experience the presence and action of God, who enters the soul, enlightening it, and enlarges the heart.

That is the description, given us by St Gregory, the great master of the interior life, of the contemplation that the Christian ascetic desires and must attain. It is the land promised to whoever follows Jesus Christ and "leaves the world" with him. These moments of high contemplation and experience of the presence of God are not necessarily accompanied by extraordinary phenomena visible to others. God gives his consolations to those who seek him seriously and perseveringly, to give comfort and strength, so that with renewed energy we will continue the strenuous task of ascetic life, which will lead us to the eternal beatific vision of the Creator.

CHAPTER 8
Liturgy and Personal Devotion

THE LITURGY IS THE PRAYER OF THE Church and the school of Christian prayer. Despite this, many Christians cannot manage to reconcile the liturgy and personal prayer. So it would be useful to say something specifically about the relationship of these two, in view of their great importance in the development our interior life. The current liturgical renewal lends additional point to this question.

Imbalance between liturgy and personal prayer shows itself in two different ways: either there is a tendency to reduce personal prayer, while celebrating the liturgy of the Divine Office with greater solemnity — or even pomposity — or else the Divine Office is subordinated to personal piety and is reduced to the indispensable minimum, and people abandon themselves to devotions which have nothing to do with the spirit of the liturgy. This can even reach the stage of regarding the Holy Mass as simply the exercise of the priest's wonderful power to consecrate, and so reducing it to a simple mechanism for obtaining a sacred host for exposition afterwards, for adoration and visits by the faithful. Both of these are errors.

A complete suppression of personal prayer outside the liturgical offices of the Church will never be part of a programme of liturgical renewal, though it is true that certain champions of the liturgy have set themselves against that half-hour of meditation which seems to have become a general practice for all religious and priests. Their goal, even so, was not a general disapproval of every exercise of meditation outside the liturgy. Their basic criticism was aimed at the watertight compartmentalisation between private prayer and the great sacrificial idea which is at the centre of worship, and the unfolding cycle of the mysteries. Another aspect of this can be an unintentional devaluing of personal prayer. It is quite true that liturgical worship, because it involves attention, even to external things, can in practice lead to formalism, and reduce, if not suppress, the true spirit of prayer. Certainly none of this is in harmony with the spirit of the liturgy, which is always primarily prayer, even if it is very solemnly celebrated. In particular, sacred chant aims to implant the riches of the thoughts embedded in the sacred texts more deeply into the human heart, to foster praying over them. It is obvious enough that liturgical celebrations reduced to the minimum length of time and substance will fail to produce such an effect. Words and rites succeed one another with such speed that they cannot make their way into the heart, never mind bear fruit there; it is not uncommon for such celebrations to become a ridiculous, and even sometimes a regrettably scandalous sight. Is that really *sentire cum Ecclesia*, following the mind of the Church? The Church views the sacraments as sacred signs which of themselves must produce grace. But the sign must always be understood by rational man, and so the Church has enriched liturgical celebrations with prayers, chants and rites. Any falsely sumptuous celebration of the liturgy, turning it into some sort of show or musical concert uninspired by piety or austerity, would be incompatible with true prayer and would certainly be contrary to the spirit of the liturgy. For the ancient writers, it was impossible to have a liturgical celebration without personal prayer. For example, St Benedict, one of the great advocates of liturgical prayer, does not suppress personal prayer. Quite the opposite, he speaks of it explicitly, seeing it as each monk's personal private continuation of the common liturgical prayer. If a monk wants to continue his prayer in private after the celebration of the Office, St Benedict sets out the requirements to ensure that he is not disturbed by others, "Once the Divine Office is over, let all go out in perfect silence in reverence to God, so that if some brother wishes to pray on his own, he may not be impeded by another's thoughtlessness."[1] In the same way, his encouragement "to give oneself frequently to prayer"[2] relates to private prayer, since the Rule itself minutely regulates common prayer. There is no point in adding other patristic testimonies to show how highly esteemed was the practice of personal prayer.

---

1 RB 52:5
2 RB 4:56

As we said, the opposite excess is the reduction of liturgical celebration to the minimum and its subordination to a personal devotion which seems to be inspired by different ideas from those which drive the liturgy. This can happen quite easily, and one can even encounter it in the lives of some saints. We know that some were dispensed from the common prayer because their mystical union was incompatible with it and with regulations laying down external behaviour. St Philip Neri found it impossible to recite his Breviary alone, since his mystical union snatched him up into such ecstasies that he was unable to continue with his vocal prayer. St Ignatius Loyola, inflamed with deep devotion, needed an hour for his celebration of holy Mass.

A modern author tries to justify such phenomena in this way: just as the obligation of the Eucharistic fast ceases in case of illness, so an extremely intimate union with God may be sufficient reason for being dispensed from common prayer.

This would obviously only be true of saints canonized by the Church, whose sanctity is not open to doubt. One cannot say, all the same, that such manifestations of piety are to be unreservedly approved, and certainly such cases are to be seen as exceptions, rather than offered to the faithful as examples for imitation. The common recitation of the Divine Office is one of the chief duties of religious, and the celebration of the holy Mass is primarily an act of collective worship rather than of personal devotion.

Furthermore, the famous investigation made by Fr Poulain, the author of *The Graces of Interior Prayer* into the incompatibility or otherwise of mystical union and liturgical prayer, shows how truly exceptional are the phenomena about which we have just been telling. On the basis of the replies received by the author, it seems clear that, even allowing for modern ideas and religious experiences, liturgical prayer recited in common does not get in the way of holy personal conversation with God. The minor difficulties which, according to these reports, may arise in reconciling the two, can easily be overcome. As others state, one can recite the Office materially, while simultaneously retaining mystical union. But does such a suggestion not already demonstrate a certain disharmony between personal prayer and liturgical prayer? Is it possible to imagine St Augustine reciting the psalms materially while thinking about something else in his heart?

Those difficulties which are sometimes met with in seeking to harmonize liturgy and personal prayer probably arise from the fact that the central idea of the liturgy differs from that of personal devotion. Therefore it seems a good idea to discover what modern people think is the central idea of personal devotion, and then compare it with that of the liturgy.

* * *

The centre of Christian piety is always the Eucharist, but that sacrament can be seen from several angles. Modern piety has often viewed the Eucharist no longer as a sacrifice, but more as simply the real presence of Jesus Christ. Many people much more willingly take part in solemn exposition of the Blessed Sacrament than the Mass, and find it more to their taste. The idea of sharing in the sacrifice has receded into the background. It is not our business to investigate the reasons for this preference, still less to pass judgement on them; we will limit ourselves to stating what others have already said on the subject. People have got into the habit of thinking of our relationship with God as something more immediate, without taking sufficient account of the sacrifice of Jesus Christ as the only way that leads to the Father. Communion itself has often been looked on as a means to union with a divine person, rather than as the sacrificial Banquet. Obviously this does not amount to a real error, nor does it involve the complete omission of an essential element of our religion; simply, less importance is being given to what ought to be at the centre of Christian consciousness. It should however be recognized that this does progressively contribute to directing the thought of the faithful towards God present on our altars. That has resulted in increased awareness of the presence of God in general, of which the Eucharist is a particular mode of presence, in which both the divinity and the humanity of our Saviour are present. In this way, the "presence of God" has gained great importance in the personal devotion of many Christians. Many treatises on mysticism and practical instruction on ascesis insist on this as a fundamental doctrine on which the entire interior life is built. This truth of God's presence everywhere is further reinforced by that of the indwelling of the three divine Persons in the souls of the faithful, as Sacred Scripture bears witness.

That God is present in all things is an undeniable truth, as also is the truth of the indwelling of the three divine persons in the souls of the righteous. It is also certain that these truths are most important for the interior life of every Christian — but are they, truly speaking, the fundamentals truths of Christian piety? Would it not be necessary to define them more clearly, to apply them to the interior life?

Some pagan philosophers, let it be noted, have taught the ascent towards God of the human spirit, and of the necessity, if that is to come about, of freeing oneself from material and passing things. Some of them have made use of the idea of divine omnipresence for this purpose. Even if their doctrine does not entirely escape from pantheistic and dualistic ideas, it is nonetheless true that their ideas were based on their conviction that God was present in the human soul. It would be necessary for the human soul to free itself from earthly attachments so as to become more like the purely spiritual and unmoved divine essence and thus achieve mystical union. Are we to think that this ascetical and mystical teaching, more or less reason-based, to some extent influenced some ecclesiastical authors? Just as many other ancient authors did, they may well have made use of such ideas, purified of their pantheist and dualist content, in order to sketch out a method of making easier the union of the spirit with God. If that is the case, they unfortunately made the mistake of thinking that the sacramental life was simply one "means", among so many others, to sanctification and purification. That would also certainly explain why the Eucharist is sometimes seen, not so much as the sacrifice of Jesus Christ, but more especially as the sacrament which makes present a divine person who is the object of our adoration and desire for union. One could sum up this view by saying that such an ascetico-mystical life would be founded on a rather rationalistic and naturalistic concept of our relationship with God. Revealed teaching and sacramental practice are no longer fundamental to it, but simply fulfil, at a higher level, an ideal which owes its chief inspirations to human reason.

Such ideas necessarily result in the Eucharistic devotion which some have called "mysticism of the tabernacle". People seeking God find him personally present on the altars, adore him, make him the friend of their souls and unite themselves to him in Holy Communion—but this is an inadequate view of the Eucharist. The liturgy takes its inspiration from ideas different from those of presence in the tabernacle and the friend of our souls. That is why, if a soul brought up on these ideas were to take liturgical texts and meditate on them and try to draw spiritual nourishment from them, unless they were helped, would be unable to overcome the difficulties which get in the way of harmonizing personal piety and sacramental life. It is true that this would bring about a certain degree of contact with the ideas of the liturgy, but it would not avoid the danger of subordinating liturgical piety to the kind of personal devotion which is not based on the fundamental truth of the sacramental life.

The importance given to the notion of the Eucharist as "presence of God" has also led, among other consequences, to people paying less attention to the reading of Sacred Scripture. For the ancients, it was one of the chief ways of coming into contact with Jesus Christ, the Word of God. In it they found Christ "present", obviously not in the same sense as in the Eucharist, and if they wished to unite themselves to Jesus Christ, to be "fed" by him, they simply went to the sacred text. While for them the Eucharist remained a means of uniting themselves to Christ, this was more by sharing, in the most concrete way, in his death and resurrection. Further, the simple notion of the presence of Christ led them to think of their brothers and sisters, members of Jesus Christ, who are always present to all of us, and they went to visit Him in the sick and the poor; they welcomed Him in pilgrims, believing that word of the Lord Himself, "Every time you did something for one of the least of these my brothers, you did it to me" (Mt. 25:40).

* * *

Liturgy and Personal Devotion

The thought which dominates the whole of the liturgy and the sacramental life is that of our sharing in Jesus Christ's sacrifice. But this participation is not a more or less external presence, as though the faithful at Mass were kneeling before the Cross to be present at the Offering of the Saviour. Taking part in the liturgy, especially if we complete it by receiving Holy Communion, is a much more real union. St Augustine, followed by the Catechism of the Council of Trent, rightly says of the Eucharistic bread that, rather than becoming part of the one who eats it, it has the power to transform the faithful who receives it into itself. The Christian is transformed into Christ, absorbed into him, sacramentally lifted up to his glorious state; dying to the world, and through Jesus Christ as intermediary becomes united to the Heavenly Father. Anyone who shares in this supernatural nourishment through the sacrament of the Eucharist thus foretastes his future perfection, which is to say his *perfect* union with Jesus Christ, which is prevented by our continuing dwelling in this world. Through it in some sense he also anticipates our physical death, insofar as in it our body of sin dies, a death which begins at baptism and continues through each one's ascetical life, until our physical death brings it to its conclusion. In the Eucharist we already undergo that death which we have not yet reached, that death that one day will definitively free us from our sinful body. As the Scholastics say, the death of Christ is *applied* to us. Jesus transforms us into himself, giving us a share in his victory over the flesh and over sin; as the Eucharist brings about in us the effects of the death and resurrection of Christ, it also makes us share in the glorious state of our Head and in his perfect spiritualisation. These are the effects of Communion. The Eucharistic bread makes whoever receives it like itself, by making the recipient a sharer in the blessed death and glorious resurrection of Jesus Christ. As we have said before, in this way the faithful anticipates that state awaiting him after his physical death and his entry into the heavenly homeland.

The fundamental notion of the liturgy is thus identical to the one which forms the basis of the life of prayer and ascesis. We have seen how the ascetic life is based on imitation of Jesus

Christ; that the ascetic separates from the world of sin in order to become a pilgrim with his Master. The life of prayer, too, is an imitation of Jesus; it is a return of the soul to the Heavenly Father, following Christ whose return, in his Ascension to heaven, precedes ours. The sacramental life does not add any further notion to what the ascetic has in mind, quite the opposite, since it is demonstrably the indispensable ontological foundation of what he proposes. Ascesis and prayer are the "natural" continuation of what the sacrament has set in motion.

* * *

If this is indeed the fundamental notion of the liturgy, if the sacramental life is indeed what supports the imitation of Christ in ascesis and prayer, then it is easy to see why there can be no opposition between the sacramental liturgical life and personal piety, except in the case where one or other of them were not properly founded on their authentic base. The liturgical life, far from suppressing ascetic effort and the spirit of personal prayer, demands both of these, since they are its necessary consequences and final development. Ascetic effort and personal prayer echo the sacramental life in the soul of each one of the faithful. If one thought that complete sanctification could be achieved by means of the sacrament alone, by common prayer alone, without ascetic effort or personal prayer, that would be a misunderstanding of the *opus operatum*, the operative sign. If we seek fruitful participation in the Eucharist, if we wish for harmony between liturgical life and prayer-life, it is necessary not merely to be convinced of this fundamental notion, but also constantly to bear it in mind. The thought that the effect of the sacrament is truly a real sharing in Christ's sacrifice, in his Passion and Resurrection, should become second nature to us and permeate all our thinking. It is not enough to receive Holy Communion and then go on to a personal prayer which is not inspired by the reality which the Eucharist brings about in us, or which is limited to the presence of Jesus Christ in our soul. Personal prayer must instead be based on that fundamental notion, that truth, that we are united to Jesus Christ in his death; that we accept constant mortification, our whole life long, but also that, at the same time, we possess the seed of our future resurrection in glory. Our whole intellectual life should be shot through with that thought; it would be the best possible preparation for reaching the most intimate union with God.

Eucharistic communion detaches man from the world and from things of earth by uniting him to Jesus Christ. He is no longer his own, but has become, even more strongly, a member of the Heavenly Jerusalem, united to Christ by the Eucharistic sacrifice, he is out of this world and already has a share in the new world to come.

* * *

The Eucharist is therefore the foundation of the ascetic and monastic life. For the ascetic, this results in the need to show in his outward attitude the separation which the Eucharist has already brought about in his soul. Through a life of mortification he continues and extends the mystical death which sacramental participation in the death of Jesus Christ began in him. Through contemplation he increases in himself the same Eucharistic reality, meditating not only on the real presence of Jesus Christ, but also and indeed primarily, on his death and Resurrection. There the ascetic finds the necessary support for his daily life, a sure guide in tribulation and an unfailing source of consolations.

Just as the Eucharist is mortification's foundation, so equally is it martyrdom's foundation, for martyrdom is simply a complete imitation of the death of Jesus Christ. That is why the ancients quite rightly considered sharing in this sacrament to be the best possible preparation for martyrdom. They had understood that whoever sacramentally shares in the death of Jesus must be ready to give external witness to the grace he has received; the fact that the Christian fortifies himself with the Eucharist expresses, one might say, a wish truly to follow his Lord, even in externals, even to the death of the cross. *Sacramenta efficient quod significant*, the sacraments bring about what they signify; this theological principal is most fully verified in martyrdom, and the deacon Laurence was expressing a profound truth when he said, seeing his bishop ready to offer the sacrifice of his own blood, that he too should be present to offer it with him; the bishop had always been assisted by his deacon when offering the Eucharistic sacrifice, and so he should also accompany him in the sacrifice of martyrdom.

Lastly, the Eucharist is the foundation of the mystical life and the life of prayer, the moving force which should lift the soul up from this world to bring it to God. Our union to Jesus Christ necessarily implies following him and truly begins this ascent.

Three kinds of holiness are united in the Eucharist: the martyr's, the ascetic's and the mystic's. All three are in the same way based on sacramental sharing in the death and resurrection of Jesus Christ, while each goes on to develop, each in its own way that sacramental seed.

Here we are particularly concerned with the relationships between the Eucharist and the life of prayer, since we find in them the justification for the idea that the life of prayer is both an ascent towards God and a separation from the world. A man of prayer belongs to two worlds, the one in which he is still living and which he will not entirely quit until his bodily death, and the other world to which he raises himself up through meditation and contemplation of the divine. A life of prayer, directed in accord with the fundamental notion of the sacrament, becomes its true continuation. Seen in that way, it will always be in harmony with liturgical life. Still more, the liturgical life and the life of prayer are surprisingly and mutually helpful and bring about a balance in the Christian life which helps in its development.

* * *

The thought of the divine guest present in the soul falls into place in a life of prayer like this, though fear of God will always remain the uppermost thought. That does not exclude the thought of the presence of God, quite the contrary, but it makes that presence desired not on account of a somewhat philosophical notion of the divine presence, nor even on account of the revealed truth of the indwelling of the three divine persons in the human soul, but rather through a strengthened conviction of our "immersion" in the death of Jesus Christ.

So the predominant thought is not that of God present, but rather — and this is the truly Christian element — the thought of a very close union with Jesus Christ our Redeemer, our "way" of going to the Father. The thought of the three divine persons does not here remain on an abstract level, but rather moves on to consideration of the real and concrete relationships of the human soul with these three persons. Let us explain.

In his long chapter seven, on humility, and which contains a complete ascetical teaching (since it shows the way to the deepest union with God), St Benedict begins by insisting on the need for fear of God. In our own day, a master of spirituality might perhaps base the spiritual ladder and the ascetico-mystical climb on the doctrine of the presence of God; St Benedict, on the contrary, sets out from the starting-point of the imminence of the Judgement. The monk should constantly keep this fear in mind, and ceaselessly think of the eternal verdict. Whatever he is doing, he should bear in mind the thought of God the Judge, scrutinizing men's hearts. The thought of the presence of God is there, but it is of God as always-present judge, and this will lead to salutary fear in the soul of the ascetic.

It should be enough to recall the Scriptural accounts: when God reveals himself to men, to show his works and his presence among them, through a miracle or some extraordinary intervention, we see those who witness these deeds filled with fear. This is not limited to the Old Law, the religion of [reverential] fear, since the Evangelists also tell how people are overcome by fear when Jesus reveals his divinity, even when they are upright and righteous: "When the crowds saw it, they were filled with awe, and they glorified God, who had given such authority to men" (Mt. 9:8). "Amazement seized all of them, and they glorified God" (Lk. 5:26). "Fear seized all of them, and they glorified God" (Lk. 7:16). It would be hard to imagine any other reaction from people, if one bears in mind how much of a contrast there is between the absolute holiness of God and the sin and misery of men.

Fear, then, is so to speak the "natural" reaction of man in the presence of God and his deeds. But the sacrament of the Eucharist puts us into immediate contact with our Saviour's divine person and his redeeming action. So is it surprising that anyone who is profoundly convinced of this truth, as a result of continual contemplation of what this sacrament brings about in his own soul, should be seized with fear, that reverential fear which stimulates whoever experiences it to praise and glorification of God? Fear took hold of him who was present at the death of Jesus when he saw the terrible verdict which God the Father had pronounced on account of our sins; should not a similar fear take hold of whoever shares in the Eucharist, which is the renewal of the same sacrifice of the cross, a renewal which compels every Christian, if necessary, to share in that same destiny of Christ?

Again, fear is the "natural" reaction which should arise in us as we await apocalyptic times. Just to read the prophecies of the Apocalypse and the descriptions they give of what will happen in the last times should be enough, merely by reading about them, to inspire something of that fear which will then take hold of all men. The Eucharist is the sacrament of those last times; it anticipates the consummation of all things, the end of the kingdoms of this world, the coming and the grace of the Father's everlasting Kingdom. Surely fear would be the spontaneous reaction of anyone facing these awe-inspiring truths?

So fear is a reaction which frequent communion will engender in anyone who considers it as it really is. It should now be obvious why the sacrament of the Eucharist needs to be seen as a good deal more than just as the only way to enter into direct contact with Christ Jesus; we also need to take into account its deep meaning as renewal of the sacrifice of the cross, of sharing in the death of Jesus and his glory and finally as anticipation of the life to come. It is the sacrament which day after day renews in us the desire for martyrdom, to which we may perhaps be called, as a testimony to our Christian life and our union with Jesus Christ. All that should arouse and maintain in us a holy fear, the same fear which St Benedict requires as the first condition for an ascetic life. Let us leave aside the question of the different kinds of fear — servile fear or filial fear, and so on. It is clear that a faithful soul cannot limit itself to fear motivated only by the desire to avoid the condemnation of the Sovereign

Judge; the over-riding fear will be filial fear, which can fit in very well with fear of eschatological happenings. God is not less our Father, despite the fact that he will one day judge us, and the tremendous sacrifice of the Cross simultaneously shows the mercy and tenderness of the Father who saves his faithful children; amidst the terrifying majesty of the events of the Apocalypse, are also to be found the Father's hand of blessing, ready to save his children from every danger and support them in tribulation.

If fear is one of the fruits of the Eucharist, it is also the basis of a personal piety in perfect harmony with the sacramental life; as we have said, it is not opposed to the practice of the presence of God, but directs it by leading us to see God as the judge to whom we will have to give an account. We come before him as sinners, but as sinners already marked by (*signati*), and who will be saved (*salvandi*), by their sharing in the death and resurrection of Jesus Christ. This fear of God, which does not exclude the practice of a life in the divine presence, likewise does not exclude the other ordinary practices of modern Eucharistic piety, such as visits to the Blessed Sacrament. The underlying thought of the sacramental life nonetheless gives these practices a new and deeper meaning, in as much as it is not primarily a matter of going and visiting God as a "prisoner" in our tabernacles, so much as renewing the sentiments which participation in this awe-inspiring sacrament arouses, personal union with the sacrificed victim, or, in a word, the fear which such participation arouses. Following the same train of thought, the altar is not the throne of a God who dwells among us, but rather it remains what it really is, the altar of the divine holocaust. In this way the notion of our union with Jesus Christ and his sacrifice, our participation in his death and glorification, can put down roots into our hearts, and such thoughts as these will sanctify our daily lives, with their joys and sorrows.

The fear that results from our participation in the sacramental life does indeed mark the first step in man's Christian life, and more especially in the ascetic life, it is always true to say, *initium sapientiae timor Domini*, the beginning of wisdom is fear of the Lord. But perfection, on the contrary, is incompatible with fear, which in the perfect ascetic has blended into charity, the result of complete conformity with the divine will.

* * *

When speaking of prayer in general, we have described the three degrees of prayer which, in order to reach union with God, make up the three subjects on which to meditate during contemplation: the external world, then our nature and finally God. These three notions should in turn be imbued with the fundamental notion of the liturgy. In this way, when contemplating the things of this world, we will place less emphasis on their transitory character (which is natural to them) and think more about the destruction and transformation which they will undergo at the end of time on account of the sin which rules the world. This view is also entirely Eucharistic in character, because the celebration of the Eucharist sacramentally brings about both our total separation from this world destined for destruction and our entry into the new world, kingdom of the Father and his angels. An ancient Eucharistic prayer, the Didache, said, "May your grace come and may the world pass away." So celebrating the Eucharist should lead man to think of the end of this material world, because it is the preparation for the world to come.

This same thought also inspires the Didache's prayer for the Church, which is at present, until Christ's second coming, bound to this world: "Remember your Church, Lord, and deliver her from every ill; give her perfection in your charity, and gather her from the four winds to make her holy in the Kingdom which you have prepared for her." In this world, the Church is scattered, she has no peace and is always suffering all sorts of ills; only at the end of time will she be set free. Persevering meditation on these truths makes it possible to grasp the true value to be set upon the exterior world and supplies the key to understanding the facts of the history of humanity and the Church. That gives the Christian soul the peace it needs to detach itself from the things of earth and commit itself entirely to those of the world beyond. This also brings the contemplation of the state of our own soul down to a more concrete level.

A man obsessed by Eucharistic truth and filled with a holy fear of God will often think about his own weakness, his sins, the judgement to come; he will dwell on the fact that he has been freed from sin and made a sharer in Christ's sacrifice. Through that sharing he will more easily attain ecstasy, overcome himself and be victorious over his sinful nature.

Meditation on the things of God is not to be limited to the divine essence, its properties and relations with the three divine persons of the Trinity, which seem to have no relevance for daily life. A man who takes the reality of the Eucharist as his starting point will find himself led to the Father through Jesus Christ as intermediary, from the very first instant that he becomes a member of his mystical body. This will anchor the notions of his personal piety and link them closely to the notion of the sacramental life, lived out day by day. Such an interior life is best nourished by the texts of Sacred Scripture and the Liturgy which, quite specially in the Psalms, its prayers, and above all in the Eucharistic Prayers, express the ideas on which the sacramental reality is founded.

* * *

Permit us to touch on another aspect of this life of personal prayer, one which was greatly honoured by ancients authors and is closely related to what we have been saying.

Everyone knows how important was prayer with tears, and the gift of tears in general, in the minds of the ancients. St Benedict also recommends that his monks accompany their prayers with tears, and still today the Roman Missal retains a prayer to ask the gift of tears[3]. The ancients thought this was the most perfect way of praying, because it was the result of a very deep consciousness and experience of the seriousness and responsibilities of the Christian life, of our personal unworthiness, fear of the end-times and of desire to see Christ return and set his Church free. These tears are not to be confused with those resulting from sentimentalism, or even from a particularly

---

3   RB 4:57. Cf. *Missale Romanum*, Editio typica altera (2002), p. 1140: Missae Ad Diversa, 38. Pro Remissione Peccatorum, B (Aliae orationes); Collect, Super Oblata and Post Communion all mention tears.

striking joy or sorrow. St Gregory the Great distinguishes them very clearly in his life of St Benedict. He tells that after having a vision of the future destruction of his monastery, he began to weep, but not, his biographer adds, in the way he habitually did during prayer, but out of sadness.[4]

The gift of tears which originates in a profound experience of the reality of the Christian life is closely related to the sacramental life, especially to the sacrifice of the Cross, which the Eucharist renews. How could one not weep at the realization of what expiation was necessary in the Eucharist for our sins, at perceiving the severity of the divine judge, at the thought of our destiny bound to that of Jesus Christ? This leads the Fathers to speak of this gift as a sign of the Holy Spirit's hold on the soul, the purifying Spirit of the world to come. It is the sign of mystical experience, of the fact that already on this earth man has begun to belong to the future world of the Kingdom of God, and through the sacrament of the Eucharist indeed realizes it most fully. Tears, then, do not come simply from the experience of our own unworthiness, from the thought of the present world, bound for destruction, and the imminence of the last judgement. They are also due to the very sweet experience of our being lifted up into the world of God, the supernatural world, where all over the Church, despite all the persecutions, the Kingdom of glory is developing, and the hour for our definitive liberation is approaching.

So the ancients were right to think of the gift of tears as a sign of a high level of prayer, a clear sign of the mystical life itself and simultaneously of salutary fear and perfect charity. It is a gift which presupposes experience of those realities which we have acknowledged as the foundations of the sacramental life. It is a state of prayer which every ascetic should desire, which so many of the Church's saints have reached, and still reach today.

It is very profitable for our interior life and our piety if we found it on the liturgy and the foundational principles which run all through it. If one gives serious and sustained attention to meditating on these, they will result in the soul experiencing

---

4 *Dial.*, II, 17:1, p. 85

a profound fear of God; they will bring about a much more realistic understanding of the meaning of the three degrees of prayer and will lead to the gift of tears, which is an indication of having mystical experience of these realities. Ten years after his conversion, St Augustine himself still remembered the powerful impression left on him by the liturgical solemnities of the Church in Milan, and gives us the following testimony,

> How I wept from the powerful emotions aroused in me by the sweetly-echoing voices of your Church, by the hymns and by the canticles. The sounds entered my ear and your truth melted my heart which burned with devotion and affection; tears fell from my eyes and gave me great joy.[5]

---

5 Augustine, *Confessions*, 9:6., trans. F. J. Sheed (Sheed & Ward, London, 1954), p. 151.

CHAPTER 9

Holy Scripture

IT IS IMPOSSIBLE TO BASE ONE'S PRAYER-life on the liturgy unless one has a deep understanding of the reality of humanity's state under the hold of sin. Our modern mind-set needs to be formed to this point of view, which the ancients reached through constant meditation of the Holy Scriptures. Scripture is also the best way of leading us into the thought of the supernatural world, so necessary for the development of the life of prayer. Sacred Scripture will not produce this effect upon our soul unless, like the bread of the Eucharist, it is regularly fed this diet, day by day.

The ancient authors saw a close relationship between the Eucharist and Sacred Scripture. Origen, for example, says,

> You are in the habit of attending the holy mysteries, and you know very well with what great care and respect you should take care of the Body of Our Lord which you receive, so as not to lose any fragment, so that none of what has been consecrated should fall on the ground. Well then, do you think it is any less a crime to treat the word of God negligently, than his body?[1]

Holy Scripture must then have a very special dignity if it is compared to the Eucharist and if it deserves a reverence equal to that due to the Body of Our Lord. A quick overview of the thought of several Fathers on the matter will make this easier to understand, it will then become obvious how necessary it is for the interior life that we read it, and how profitable is that reading.

* * *

Holy Scripture is called the "Word of God". The Son of the Father, the second person of the Holy Trinity, is also called "Word of God". The fact that they share the same name shows

---

[1] Origen, *Hom. in Exod.*, 13, 3: *Origen, Homilies on Genesis and Exodus*, translated by Ronald E. Heine, FOTC Vol. 71 (CUA Press, 1982), pp. 380–81.

the intimacy of the relationship existing between the consubstantial Word of God and the word of God contained in the Scriptures. If the Word Incarnate is our only salvation, then the written Word of God must share the same dignity.

St John begins his Gospel, "In the beginning was the Word, and the Word was with God, and the Word was God" (Jn. 1:1). This is the primary text on the Word of God, and we know how important it was in the long debates on the mystery of the Holy Trinity. It makes clear that our God is not an isolated God, but a God who lives in an eternal communion of person with his Word, his Son. The Son, as Word and as Word of the Father, makes the Father manifest; he is the word who communicates him. The God who possesses such a Word, himself communicates such a Word. The eternal and co-natural Word is the one whom God the Father expresses by nature, and that Word comes to us through the Incarnation. Every other revelation of the Father must be modelled on this first, eternal, infinitely perfect Word, and must in some way share in it. The Word of God to be found in the Holy Scriptures is an especially faithful reproduction of it; Sacred Scripture is a Word of God, it speaks to us of God; like the Word Incarnate, it reveals divine mysteries to us. There is to be found its first relationship with the Word of God.

But there is a further relationship, arising from the fact that Scripture speaks to us of the Word himself. It is inspired by the Holy Spirit, true enough, but it does not however contain the Holy Spirit, but the Word. Everything that Holy Scripture says, every word of Holy Writ, has a relationship with the Divine Word. Anyone who reads Holy Scripture without seeing that, anyone who seeks something else in it, is closing himself off from real understanding of the sacred text. In every book of Scripture, there is nothing else to be found except what relates to the incarnate Word: in other words, the story of our salvation. Read from any angle but that, the Holy Scriptures — especially the Old Testament — have very little to say. The Psalms, the historical books, the Prophets, at base they speak only of man's salvation, the work of the Redemption and of the Word of God Incarnate. This was what Augustine meant when he wrote,

Read all the prophetic books; if you have not found Christ there, what could be more tasteless and empty? See Christ there, and then not only will you savour what you read, you will be inebriated by it; detach your spirit from material things, so as to forget the past, and aspire to future things.[2]

So Holy Scripture always speaks of Christ, the Word of God, and so possesses a most intimate relationship with the second Divine Person. But it is also bound to the Word in still another meaning, for whoever wishes to understand it must themselves be full of the Word of God and by grace possess him in their soul. That was what Origen meant, when he said that only one who rests on the breast of Jesus can understand the Gospel of St John, in other words, someone who is personally intimate with the Incarnate Word.[3] No one can grasp the true meaning of the Gospel unless led into it by Him of whom the Evangelist said, "He opened their minds to understand the Scriptures" (Lk. 24:45).

Holy Scripture is the Word of God, just as is the Word Incarnate. It speaks to us of Christ and can only be understood through him. It is not a human book, and understanding it presupposes a spirit lifted up, enlightened by grace and united to the Word of God. If Christ is absolutely necessary for our salvation, how can Scripture, which is also the Word of God, not also be so?

* * *

The Word of God incarnate continues to live and act in the Church, so Holy Scripture refers to the Church in a quite special way. The Catholic faith teaches that it is she who gives the true interpretation of Scripture to the faithful, and this follows logically from the fact that Scripture is the word of God. Words are not merely to be read but are primarily meant to be

---

2 Augustine, *On John* 9, 3, (2): *Tractates on the Gospel of John 1–10*, translated by John W. Rettig, FOTC Vol. 78 (CUA Press 1988), p. 197.
3 Origen, *On John* I, 6; *Origen: Commentary on the Gospel According to John*, Books 1–10, translated by Ronald E. Heine, FOTC Vol. 80 (CUA Press, 1989).

heard. The written word contained in the sacred scriptures must be "spoken" in order to be heard, because the written word is not a complete word. The doctors of the Church are the ones by whose mouths this written word reaches us and gains new life — though "doctors" is not a description limited to those who have after their death, for their notable explanations of Christian teaching, received this title from the Church; rather and above all it means those among us entrusted with the task of teaching revealed doctrine, the bishops and priests. The responsibility of pasturing the Lord's flock has been given to them, distributing their daily bread to the faithful, interpreting the Scriptures, as the Lord did with his disciples. If Scripture contains our spiritual daily bread, if it is incumbent on priests to break it and distribute it to the faithful, should we be surprised if the supernatural life of the Church is less perfect than we might wish? Should the reason perhaps be sought in the fact that priests are failing in their duty? How many devotional deviations might have been avoided if Scripture had been the accustomed nourishment of faithful souls!

Already in St John Chrysostom's day, he found himself obliged to persuade his faithful of their duty to read Scripture and to convince them that not being monks was not enough to excuse them from it. "Some of you say, 'I'm not a monk, I have a wife and children, I have to look after my household.' But you are wrong there," he says,

> in thinking that reading Scripture is only for monks, when in fact it is all the more necessary for you, because you live amidst the world and every day receive wounds that need bandaging. If there is one thing worse than not reading Scripture, it's believing that reading Scripture is useless — that is how Satan speaks.[4]

On another occasion he goes on to explain how people should practise reading at home:

---

4 Chrysostom, Homilies on Matthew, 2, 10; *The Homilies of S. John Chrysostom, On the Gospel of Matthew*, translated with notes and indices. Part I. Hom. I–XXV (Oxford, John Henry Parker, Rivingtons, London, 1852), p. 27.

Holy Scripture

Having got back from church, the husband should go over what was read; his wife will learn it, his children will listen to it, his servants will not be deprived of it, and in that way, as well as the material table, the spiritual table will be prepared.[5]

Priests and those in the Church whose responsibility it is to teach should not rely on their personal judgement alone in explaining Scripture. Scripture has been given to the whole Church, and so it needs to be understood in the sense that the Church understands it, by knowing the teaching of the Church's tradition and following its mind. That is why it is not enough, at least for the priest and theologian, simply to read the sacred text, they also need to consult the commentaries and interpretations of the holy Fathers. They are rightly called Fathers, because by their teaching they give spiritual life, because they are authentic interpreters of Scripture, endorsed by the Church's tradition.

It is nonetheless clear that reading the commentaries of the Fathers cannot replace the reading of Holy Scripture. Further, there are many points in which we can neither follow the Fathers' interpretations nor accept their explanations, for they were explaining the Scriptures for the faithful of their times, and we have to interpret and understand it in accordance with our own times. That does not mean to say that the doctrine has changed or that we ought to understand it differently today; yes, it is unchanging, but it is also so rich that it is inexhaustible and cannot be limited to the needs of a single specific era. It speaks to every age, and must be read in every era, because it responds to the needs of every age, whatever they may be, and to what is necessary for every epoch. All the same, by reading the Fathers' commentaries we enter more deeply into the spirit of the Catholic tradition and learn to grasp the relationships which unite the various books of the Old and New Testament, the relationships between doctrine and history in Scripture, and above all the relationship to current events, so that we learn

---

5   Chrysostom, *On Ephesians*, sermon 20 (PG 62): *St John Chrysostom, On Marriage and Family Life*, translated by Catherine P. Roth & David Anderson (St Vladimir's Seminary Press, 1986).

to see them from a supernatural viewpoint, in other words in terms of their relationship to sin and the work of Redemption.

It is not easy to understand the Holy Scriptures in this way. It is relatively easy to give a "literal" interpretation, to establish clearly what is directly expressed in the sacred Text. That is what the Fathers mean when they speak of the "letter" of Scripture, or its historical meaning, which they insist is necessary and valuable. But they point out that this is not the only meaning; if it is deliberately given by God to meet the needs of those simple faithful who do not aspire to a higher degree of spiritual life in this world, it is nonetheless in some sense imperfect, for the sacred Text constantly alludes to the work of Redemption, the person of the Saviour, the Church and her destiny, the needs of souls on the way of the Lord and the different stages through which the soul must pass on the way of perfection. Seeing the text of Scripture from these aspects and without giving way to arbitrary subjective interpretations requires a deeper understanding than the literal sense (though that is the foundation underlying the allegorical and spiritual interpretations); it requires a special gift to be able to find the reflection of our present life in the sacred word. It is in this that the Fathers can be our masters and guides; a Catholic interpreter of Scripture who seeks to be as much in touch and as lively an interpreter for his own era as the Fathers were for theirs, also needs to be able to go beyond the literal interpretation alone, and not to limit himself exclusively to it.

So Sacred Scripture is fundamental for the spiritual life of the Church. Reaching this source of living water is not without difficulty, we need to pray to the Holy Spirit, asking light to work, study and meditate. St Augustine says,

> We should think of Holy Scripture as a field on which we want to build. So we should not be satisfied with what appears on the surface, we should not be lazy. We need to dig down till we reach the rock. Because the rock is Christ.[6]

---

6 Augustine, *On John* 23, I: *Tractates on the Gospel of John 11–27*, translated by John W. Rettig, FOTC Vol. 79 (CUA Press 1988), p. 212.

Holy Scripture

So it is necessary to seek and work until we find Christ, the true link uniting the text and our salvation and our spiritual life.

* * *

Interpreted in this way, Holy Scripture is indeed the soul's daily bread. When the Fathers talk of the soul's supernatural bread, they are not generally thinking of the Eucharistic bread, or at any rate, not of it alone, but almost always of Sacred Scripture. The Eucharist and Scripture are often set in parallel. Both were treated with respect, they were kept in similar precious containers, just like the Eucharist; the Scriptures were exposed on a sort of throne, surrounded with lights, etc.... And Scripture can be compared not only to the Eucharist, but, as we have already said, to the whole mystery of the Incarnation; and if the whole essence of our sanctification consists of following the Word Incarnate and assimilating it wherever we find it, we should likewise search in the Scriptures where he is hidden, or rather where he offers himself in a way adapted to our poor understanding: "Remember," says St Augustine,

> that it is the same Word of God who extends through all the divine Scriptures, and that it is one and the same Word which is heard in all the mouths of the sacred writers, He who in the beginning was with God, who had no need of syllables to express himself because he is not subject to time's succession. It should not surprise us if, out of consideration for our weakness, he comes down to the level of using the fragmentary syllables of our speech, since he also lowers himself to making the weakness of our body his own.[7]

Since Holy Scripture is a sort of Incarnation, it is necessary that it be adapted to our intelligences, so that it can then lift them up afterwards to the sublime heights of the divinity. This is how reading the Holy Scriptures shares in our lifting up:

---

7 Augustine, *On Psalm 103*, 4, I; Exposition 4 of Psalm 103. *The Works of Saint Augustine, A Translation for the 21st Century. Expositions of the Psalms (Enarrationes in Psalmos) 99–120*. Part III, Volume 19. Translation and notes by Maria Boulding OSB (New City Press, NY, 2003), p. 167.

> Scripture cannot lift us up unless it comes down to us, just as the Incarnate Word lowered himself in order to lift us up again, and did not fall to remain down. If we have recognized him while he is down, let us lift ourselves up again with him when he raises himself again.[8]

The parallelism between the Word incarnate and Holy Scripture goes further still. In a certain way, Scripture shares in Christ's Passion. The material and human part, the sacred text itself, has over the centuries been transformed, distorted and maltreated; even its exterior appearance, its immediate and literal meaning, can seem so human to us that it can scandalize; so it is that those who cannot see the hidden divine character of the Scriptures are scandalized by that aspect of the Bible, because they cannot grasp its sublimity. St Augustine says, "Holy Scripture has its own language, and whoever does not understand that language is troubled by it."[9] Just as faith is needed to believe in the divinity of Jesus Christ and his Church, so we need faith to give ourselves to study of Holy Scripture, to grasp its sublimity and its godly meaning, in spite of its outward covering which sometimes seems so human and humble.

So, Holy Scripture which also in a certain way shares in the Incarnation, therefore finds itself linked to the Church and the work of Redemption. It would have been unnecessary in the earthly paradise, and after the end of the world, there will likewise be no need for it.

> When...Our Lord Jesus Christ comes...when he enlightens the darkness and shows the thoughts of his own people...then in the face of the brilliance of such a sun, lamps will be useless; no one will read the prophet then, no one will explain the book of the Apostle anymore, the testimony of St John will no longer be necessary, nor even the Gospel itself. All the Scriptures will disappear.[10]

---

8 *Ibid.*, *On John*, 107, 6, (2); *Tractates on the Gospel of John 55–III*, translated by John W. Rettig, FOTC Vol. 90 (CUA Press 1994), p. 277.
9 *Ibid.*, 10, 2 (2); *Tractates on the Gospel of John 1–10*, translated by John W. Rettig, FOTC Vol. 78 (CUA Press 1988), p. 212.
10 *Ibid.*, 35, 9 (3); *Tractates on the Gospel of John 28–54*, translated by

Holy Scripture

The Scriptures, like the sacraments, are a consolation given to the Church for her time of pilgrimage; once the *parousia* and the end of all things arrive, they will lose their usefulness. But these facts emphasize all the more how important they are for life here and now, in which they are something of an anticipation of what we will one day experience, just as the sacraments are an anticipation of the life of beatitude; and so the necessity becomes clear for us to let ourselves be formed by the teachings of Scripture during this life, because it is the true food of our spirit, and it supplies our human intelligence with the knowledge and consolation it needs during the present life while awaiting the return of Christ.

* * *

Up to now, we have spoken of Scripture's dignity and its importance for the spiritual life; from this it appears that it is part of what, in the present state of things, Jesus Christ has laid down for our salvation, that it is closely related to the Incarnation and the life of the Church, and that it is to be a source of teaching and consolation until the Lord comes again.

Its immediate relationship to the sanctification of each one of use remains to be treated.

If someone who reads it interprets it correctly, that implies in them a certain degree of holiness and spiritual tranquillity, without which they would only be able to see the difficulty of the text and its apparent contradictions, all of which would prevent reading the Scripture from bearing its fruits, as St Augustine warns us, "In the Scriptures, peace reigns and all is well ordered, there is no contradiction. So you too must free your heart from disorder, and seek its harmonies. How could the truth speak against itself?"[11] That is why, besides good dispositions, we need the action of God's grace when we approach Holy Scripture, as well as our will. We need always to pray in order to understand it.

John W. Rettig, FOTC Vol. 88 (CUA Press 1993), p. 79.
11   *Ibid.*, 19,7 (3); *Tractates on the Gospel of John 11-27*, translated by John W. Rettig, FOTC Vol. 79 (CUA Press 1988), p. 145.

Moses wrote this, he wrote it and went away. He went from there to go to you, and now he is no longer before me. If he were there, I would lay hold of him, pray him, beg him in your name to enlighten me on these matters. And I would open my bodily ears in order fully to grasp the words coming from his mouth.... Since I cannot ask him, I turn to you, to Truth, towards you about whom he who was filled with you spoke truths. And I pray you, my God, I pray you, have mercy on my sins. You brought it about that your servant should say these things, grant that I too may understand them.[12]

* * *

The Scriptures are spiritual food for all. Where books on spirituality are concerned, one must carefully check to see whether this or that book is really suitable for the current state of a soul, in case reading it would do more harm than good. Contrariwise, as many of the Fathers have pointed out, we find in Holy Writ a spiritual food which really suits everyone. On this subject, St Gregory the Great, one of the greatest interpreters of Sacred Scripture, says, for example, in his commentary on Ezekiel, that the literal and historical meanings, more especially the parts containing moral teaching, are easy to understand and make excellent food for the "simple", those who do not have a well-developed spiritual life (even though they may be very full of devotion). Certain parts of Scripture are more obscure. Those who are already rather stronger, spiritually speaking, will find in that a stimulus which will lead them to work at discovering the exact interpretation and to try to discover its more profound and hidden meaning. We have only to think of the intellectual strivings of Origen or St Augustine to elucidate some of Scripture's obscurities. These passages do not suit the "simple", who cannot savour them, and pass on. St Gregory says there are even some texts of the holy books that are so obscure that no one among us will ever manage to understand them; these passages are there to try our humility. Sometimes, then, Scripture's goal is to exercise

---

12 Augustine, *Confessions* 11,3:, translated by F. J. Sheed (Sheed & Ward, London, 1954), p. 210.

Holy Scripture

us directly in the practice of virtue. And even, St Gregory thinks, for that reason, that certain things are deliberately expressed in such a way as to be unclear to all but those who already dwell above in the heavenly homeland; we, on the other hand, will never have the complete explanation while we live here below. There is one part of Scripture, then, which exercises us in virtue, particularly in humility, while that part which we can understand here and now guides our life and makes us grow in perfection.

In another place,[13] St Gregory explains the different meanings of Scripture. The first, the "simple" meaning, is the norm for the active life; even though it is still imperfect, it is nonetheless very useful. There is also the spiritual meaning, which is offered us when the text of Scripture gives us a theme and invites us to contemplate it. *Divina eloquia cum legente crescunt*, as St Gregory puts it, the divine words grow with the reader; in other words, one who is more perfect, more experienced, more spiritual, understands Scripture more deeply, penetrates further into the text and finds in it material for sublime contemplation. It may happen that the same text may mean something much simpler and less profound to another reader. That is part of the supernatural character of the Holy Scriptures, which are not limited to one and the same level of understanding.

* * *

Scripture, then, provides nourishment for every intelligence and suitable for every level of spiritual life. It nonetheless requires diligent and persevering effort, because, to begin with, everyone finds it very difficult, especially we modern Christians. We shouldn't blame the Bible, as though it were no longer suited to our age — that would be an insult to the inspired word. Our intellects no longer bear the impress of the divine Word in the same way as did the Christians of the past, and we can say that without wronging anyone. We all know that we no longer have the same familiarity with Holy Scripture as had the Christians

---

[13] St Gregory the Great, Homilies on Ezekiel: Book I, Homily 7; 8–9; *The Homilies of St. Gregory the Great On the Book of the Prophet Ezekiel*, Translated by Theodosia Gray and edited by Juliana Cownie (Centre for Traditionalist Orthodox Studies, Etna, California, 1990), pp. 68–9.

of the first centuries, for whom it was their primary spiritual nourishment. The way in which it expresses itself and the ideas it expresses are no longer as familiar to us as they were to them. Even so, Origen's classic dictum has lost none of its truth for us: *Cibus verus naturae rationabilis sermo Dei est,* the true food for a rational creature is the word of God.[14] He explains that, just as there is a great variety of foods to nourish the body, and since every food does not suit every metabolism, similarly a rational creature cannot be nourished with just any word of God. Those beginning the spiritual life, says Origen, chiefly need instructional texts.

> If you read to them a didactic text of Scripture, which does not present them with any difficulty, they will accept it willingly — things like the Book of Esther, or Judith or Tobit, or else Wisdom's teachings. But read Leviticus to them, and their heart is invaded by darkness, and they reject a food which is not meant for them.... The fault is not in Scripture, so it should not be immediately blamed or rejected because it seems too difficult and too obscure for our understanding.

For the whole of Scripture, and each one of its books, does indeed come from God, a food prepared for intelligent creatures: "Each takes as much as needed, according to their capacity." Just as animals at pasture are capable of distinguishing what is useful from what is harmful, they choose what suits them and leave the rest. Origen concludes by once more advising readers to implore God's grace,

> Let us turn the gaze of our spirit towards Him upon whose orders these things were written, and let us ask for understanding, so that He who cures every ill may cure the frailties of our soul (*sanat omnes languores ejus*). And if we only have moderate understanding, may the Lord who protects the weak (*custodiens parvulos*) help us, nourish us and bring us finally to adulthood.

---

14   Origen, *Hom. In Num.*, 27, 1, 2; *Origène, Homélies sur les Nombres, III*, nouvelle édition par Louis Doutreleau, SJ, Sources chrétiennes [SC] 461, Cerf, Paris, 2001, p. 273

Holy Scripture

* * *

All that we have said applies to reading Holy Scripture in general, whether it be the Old Testament or the New. It is understandable that every Christian will eagerly read the New Testament, but it is also necessary to read the Old Testament, which is just as much the Word of God, "for whatever was written in former days was written for our instruction" (Rom. 15:4), as "all Scripture is inspired by God, and is useful for teaching, for reproof, for correction, and for training in righteousness" (2 Tim. 3:16).

Even so, when we read the Old Testament we should not look for what is not to be found there. None of its various books supplies any philosophical teaching at all on God or on his relationship with the world. It is primarily an interpretation of historical reality that goes beyond the order of nature and of reason, and their chief object is to convey to just what extent God has lowered himself in order to communicate himself to us. The story of Paradise tells us of the beginning of that coming down to our level, of the cause of evil and of the preparation for future restoration. It is astonishing to see how the human race, after having gone so far away from God, was always gently called back by him. Each and every book develops this theme, and in each of them, everyone, especially the "simple" faithful, can find a word of life to suit them. In proportion as each advances in reading, if they are assiduous and diligent, if shot through with devotion and true compunction, then the reader will come to say with St Augustine,

> May the Scriptures be my chaste delight, so that I do not go astray in them nor lead others into error through them.... Not in vain did you will that so many obscure and mysterious pages should be written.... See, Father, look, give your approval, and may it please you that in your mercy I may find grace, so that the gates of your word may open before me, when I knock on them from outside. I entreat you through Jesus Christ Our Lord, your Beloved Son... Him whom I seek in your books.[15]

---

15 *Confessions*, 11, 2, trans. Sheed, p. 209.

CHAPTER 10

The Ascetic as Apostle

AT FIRST GLANCE, THE APOSTOLATE would seem irreconcilable with ascetic life, which by its nature tends as much as possible to avoid contact with the world, if, that is, one has in mind an ascetic life with its goal in pure contemplation which is not subordinate to a practical end. The apostolate about which we are talking should not be thought of as a certain exterior activity of the ascetic, nor should it be confused with the cenobite's pastoral activity—we spoke about that earlier. Here we are dealing with a special kind of apostolic labour, one which is proper to the *perfect* ascetic. As we know, the monks who withdrew into the desert, and hermits too, exercised an apostolate conditioned by special and carefully defined limits. What St Gregory the Great and St Benedict have to say about this is very instructive.

* * *

The story of the carnal temptation which St Benedict experienced as a young hermit in the cave at Subiaco is well known. The saint managed to overcome it thanks to an heroic act of mortification, when he threw himself into the thorns; thereafter he was never again bothered by that sort of temptation. St Gregory goes on,

> Many were they who decided to leave the world in order to place themselves under his guidance. Now that he was raised above temptations, he was indeed worthy to become a master of virtue for others. That was why the Lord ordered, through the mouth of Moses, that Levites aged more than twenty-five should serve in the temple, and that those aged over fifty should be entrusted with the custody of the sacred vessels.[1]

---

[1] *Dial.*, II, 2,3, p. 60

According to St Gregory, this enactment shows that in the New Testament's scheme of things, while they are still exposed to temptation, ministers should be placed under superiors, and should serve and wear themselves out in work. It is only with mature years, or, as in St Benedict's case, on account of extraordinary perfection in ascesis, that they will be sheltered from temptation, and thus be fit custodians of the sacred vessels, souls in other words.

St Gregory teaches here, that it is thanks to his heroic virtue that St Benedict had reached this degree of perfection, that he had become a master of the spiritual life; it was not some sort of natural aptitude that entitled him to this responsibility, to teach and direct, which were certainly not the normal, ordinary activity for a young hermit. No, it was the ripe fruit and natural consequence of preceding ascetic preparation.

Once they had reached perfection, the ancient hermits received the title of "Abba", father, and became masters for many ascetics; these Abbas and masters were not the hermits' community officials, in the modern legal meaning of the term. Unlike the other officials, they did not receive their responsibility from higher authority; rather the responsibility fell to them from the very fact of their having reached a certain degree of perfection, a fact publicly recognized in some fashion through the intermediary of the Holy Spirit. This quite special form of apostolate, "spiritual fatherhood" is the hallowed term, is a more or less spontaneous result of perfection, and is in continuity with the ascetic life. This apostolate, this spiritual fatherhood, are not essential characteristics of the ascetic on the same level as others, such as martyrdom or service in the ranks of Christ. Fatherhood is a special gift, a charism, which the ascetic cannot claim by right, even when perfection has been reached, and is the outcome of a special vocation from God. Apostolate and spiritual fatherhood presuppose that the ascetic has attained perfection, but not every perfect ascetic becomes an apostle or a spiritual father. That is why, in the Life of St Benedict, his magisterial gift is shown to us as the result of a special call from God. St Benedict had no desire to set himself up as a master of the spiritual life, but God wanted it so, because "he had arranged it so that the glory of the life of Benedict should enlighten men and be an example to them."[2]

In order fully to grasp the nature and importance of this gift of the perfect ascetic, we need to go more deeply into the notion of spiritual fatherhood.

* * *

To be a "father" is to transmit life. Life is still one of the great mysteries. If, along with some philosophers, we define life as the power "to move oneself", that limits it to only one of the ways in which it is manifested, and is simply an external description of a living being, without saying anything about what that life is in its intimate nature. That can scarcely be otherwise, since the origin of life is entirely hidden to us and transcends our spirit. The source of all life is the first person of the Holy Trinity, the Father, the first divine person, principle of the other persons, and, with them, the principle of every creature. All life flows from Him, and since none of us has seen the Father, life in its essence remains something mysterious to us, something beyond our comprehension.

It is not natural life which interests us here, but only the supernatural life which the Father transmits to us through the intermediary of the Son, our Redeemer. The Son, head of the mystical Body, is our source of supernatural life, which is grace.

This life is given to us by the sacraments, above all by the sacrament of baptism and by faith. Faith and baptism are the two indispensable conditions for possessing the life of Christ: "He who believes and is baptized will be saved" (Mk. 16:16).

The sacrament was instituted by Jesus Christ and comes to us from Him; faith transmits his teaching to us. They are both summed up in the word "faith", since baptism is the sacrament of faith. The priest asks of the one seeking baptism, "What do you want of the Church of God?", and the candidate replies, "Faith". As he is our master, Jesus Christ is the source of that life: "You call me Teacher and Lord; and you are right, for so I am," (Jn. 13:13). "Master" is the great title which he has won

---

[2] *Dial.* II, 1,6, p. 58

through the work of the Redemption. Humanity, gone astray, has found what it was looking for and had not been able to find until then: the truth and the life.

Jesus Christ is Master not only on account of his teaching, but also his example—the text from St John just quoted goes on, "If I then, your Lord and Teacher, have washed your feet, you also ought to wash one another's feet. For I have given you an example, so that you also should do as I have done to you" (Jn. 13:14-15). That is precisely what distinguishes Jesus Christ's teaching from that of the Pharisees: Jesus offers an example and practises it, whereas the Pharisees teach their doctrine and act otherwise.

Jesus Christ is indeed the ideal and complete Master, because he teaches both by word and example. Does that make him the father of our spiritual life? Certainly so, but in order to avoid confusing the divine persons, and in order to distinguish the first person, the "Father" above all, from Jesus, who is the immediate father of our spiritual life, the title "father" is rarely used of the second person. According to St Benedict, however, the abbot of the monastery bears this title because he represents Christ and his fatherhood. "He is called by the name which belongs to Jesus Christ... Abba, Father."[3]

So the title Father may also be applied to a man who may indeed exercise a true fatherhood in relation to the spiritual life. He possesses this spiritual fatherhood when, above all, he teaches the doctrine of Jesus Christ. This is what St Paul means when he says to his faithful, "For though you might have countless guides in Christ, you do not have many fathers. For I became your father in Christ Jesus through the gospel" (1 Cor. 4:15). But in a man who shares in this paternal dignity of Christ, teaching must still be linked to example, since it is Christ's fatherhood. The true spiritual father should be able to refer to his own example, on the same level as to his teaching, as the norm of conduct for his sons: "Be imitators of me, as I am of Christ" (1 Cor. 11:1). This is St Benedict's ideal, too; he thinks the Abbot's teaching should be two-fold, "That is to say that he should show, more

---

[3] RB 2:1-2

by his actions than by his words, what is good and holy."[4] A Benedictine abbot, his sons' spiritual father, is thus a true imitator of Jesus Christ; he offers example together with teaching. That is spiritual fatherhood in its perfection.

* * *

We wondered if spiritual fatherhood was compatible with a higher level of ascetic life, with a monk's life, or more especially, with the life of a hermit who seeks to have the least possible contact with the world. Is this fatherhood, like all other apostolic works, not reserved to the priesthood? Analysis of the ascetic ideal will demonstrate that there is no discontinuity between spiritual fatherhood and the ascetic life, still more because it presupposes, as we said, a certain degree of perfection and a special call from God. The following remarks will shed light on the matter.

The trend of the ascetic's life is to form Jesus Christ, the divine Word, in himself, by following and imitating Christ. He shapes his soul to the perfections of the divine Word, the first and perfect image of the heavenly Father. Christ, the ascetic's example, is "Father", and the divine Word, his supreme model, is not a silent word, not a dumb word. His word has re-echoed throughout the whole word. So why should not one who imitates Jesus Christ and the Word share in that perfection? Why should not he in turn transmit and generate life, cause the word of life to be trumpeted forth? So this privilege of transmitting supernatural life is in harmony with the ascetic life, since it is an imitation of Christ.

Another train of thought brings us to the same conclusion. The Christian ascetic is not an isolated being, he remains a member of the ecclesial community, a member of the mystical body of Jesus Christ, in which he fulfils a special function corresponding to his charism. No healthy member of this mystical body can be useless to the others. We have already noted that the ascetic is a friend of Jesus Christ and how he constantly intercedes for the rest of the faithful. The apostolate of prayer

---

[4] RB 2:12

is thus something proper to the ascetic, just as is teaching by example. It is undeniable that a community of ascetics, even lacking direct contact with the world, by the very fact of its existence exercises a very great influence on the world, and that represents a fatherhood, a gift of life, which every ascetic can and must exercise. This is not fatherhood properly so-called, since there is no direct teaching of doctrine.

The ascetic who seeks to lead a perfect Christian life also in some sense imitates Adam, our first father, when he was living in the earthly paradise in a state of high perfection. The ascetic, as we said earlier, sets out in search of paradise lost by sin. God had not destined Adam merely to be the "natural" father, as we might say, of the human race, his greatest privilege would have been to be the first teacher, the first spiritual father, of his children. That dignity Adam lost, but is now possessed by Jesus Christ, the true and second Adam, father of that human race which he redeemed. That too is within reach of the ascetic; like all the first man's other graces, it is something he can laboriously win back.

* * *

The fatherhood and the apostolate about which we are speaking presuppose a special vocation. A real ascetic does not put himself forward to become an apostle or spiritual father, but rather backs away from it, only accepting if he sees that it is clearly God's will. Since this new vocation implies a new charism for him, closely related to the other charisms of the Church, he does not become an independent entity as a spiritual father or apostle, but remains subject to the direction of those who have a higher charism; monks, in particular, will be careful not to give themselves privileges arising from such an additional vocation, so as to withdraw from obedience, even if that submission to ordinary superiors may lead to serious difficulties. Further, this apostolate can be exercised in very different ways, not only by preaching to pagans as such, but also by the pen, giving conferences and instructing.

The example of the Camaldolese supplies a confirmation of what we maintain, namely that his apostolate presupposes a special vocation in him and a high level of perfection in the conception of an order which is still flourishing today, the Camaldolese. They distinguish three degrees in religious life: the first degree, cenobitic life, then simple hermits and finally, Apostles. This apostolic life has various forms, "The soul which lives in an uninterrupted total gift of self to God has the ineffable privilege, which becomes its right, in the spiritual sense, if it puts no voluntary obstacle in the way, of truly acting upon souls." This recent apologist for the Camaldolese ideal goes on,

> This state corresponds to reclusion, the living holocaust of a life which for a set period, or until death, imprisons itself within the four walls of a cell, cut off from all contact with men, far from every consolation and human help, in a voluntarily intensified act of oblation, often pushed to beyond its limits; or again the word of God carried to the pagans, with martyrdom as the goal, or else magisterial responsibility among the brothers, as Prior or instructor.[5]

It is immediately clear that it is the desire for martyrdom, the ideal of the Christian ascetic life which characterizes this higher degree, the apostolate, and that it is reclusion, a completely hermit life, which comes closest to the martyrdom of blood, of which it is the most perfect imitation—preaching amidst the pagans and the apostolate of the word are only carried out, out of desire for that martyrdom of blood. The offices of Prior and instructor belong to this degree, which is higher than that of the simple hermit, only if they are not looked on as simply ordinary responsibilities which might be carried out by any capable and devout monk but—something rare and comparable to the case of St Benedict—as the fruit of attained perfection, the ascetic having reached the fullness of perfection. This magisterial gift testifies to a non-bloody martyrdom, essentially different from the teaching which a priest or superior gives by reason of his office. Such magisterial teaching has a quite special efficacy, because it joins the irresistible power of living example to the energy of the word of God. This apostolate and magisterium are very close to

---

[5] Anselmo Giabbani, Le fonti del pensiero camaldolese, in *Vita Cristiana*, 1941, p. 469

martyrdom, and like it presuppose a very special vocation. The Camaldolese conception thus clearly shows of what the apostolate of the perfect ascetic consists: it is not the ordinary labour of the care of souls which is the obligation reserved to the priestly life, and, with some limitations, to the monk-priest; no, it is a matter of ascetic perfection which has reached such a degree that it is exteriorized as a witness for the good of the brothers.

* * *

Spiritual fatherhood and the ascetic apostolate presuppose a living example as well as verbal teaching. That is why the teaching of a priest, pastor of souls, will be so much more effective if he adds to it the power of example. Even so, the priestly dignity, the priest's right and duty to be a pastor, is not directly related to his moral qualities. It is quite otherwise with the ascetic's apostolate, which becomes totally unreal without example, because spiritual children are not begotten by the doctrine he teaches, but also, and above all, by the way he lives his teaching, incarnated in his own life. The ancient desert ascetics shared their cell with a disciple in order to form him, first of all, by the example of their daily lives. The *Apophthegms* tell that a young man sought out an old ascetic in order to be instructed in the way of perfection, but the elder said not a word. The young man asked why he was silent. "Am I a superior, that I should give you orders?" replied the old man, "I shall say nothing. If you wish, do as you see me doing." From then on, the young man imitated the old man in everything, and all this in silence. So it was that he learned to lead the ascetic life in deep silence.[6] In the same spirit, another Abba advised a colleague who was to instruct disciples, "Be their example, not their legislator."[7]

The doctrine of the ancient Fathers supplies us with a criterion by which to judge whether an ascetic has reached perfection, and is thus fit to exercise the apostolate and to teach. The treatise on the life of St Benedict referred to earlier presupposed that the ascetic-apostle had achieved complete mastery of his passions and

---

6 *Apophthegmata Appendix ad Palladium*, on Abba Isaac, 2 (PG 65, 224D).
7 *Ibid.*, Abba Poemen 174: PG 65, 564D.

the gift of *apatheia*. Abba Pimen said, "Teaching his neighbour befits one who is healthy and free from passions. If someone is ruining his own house, how can he truly build someone else's?"[8]

This *apatheia* is the surest indicator of acquired perfection. Through it a man achieves self-mastery and reconquers the right to raise himself above the external world, just as did Adam before his fall, since the power to control other creatures was related to man's ability to control himself. That is why St Gregory emphasizes the fact that St Benedict's beginnings as a magisterial teacher were linked to his heroic victory. *Apatheia* is a further protection to the master of the spiritual life from the very grave dangers built into his responsibilities, of which the chief is vanity. If he becomes proud over the number of his spiritual sons and their progress under his guidance, if he allows his magisterial status to lift him up in any way whatsoever, then that makes it certain that he has not reached *apatheia* or perfection. His teaching will not be the kind of ascetic apostolate we are talking about.

Similarly, if the master makes use of his teaching and his disciples to serve material ends, he shows that he is still a slave to his passions, and thus an imperfect master of the spiritual life; furthermore, his behaviour is contradictory to the Lord who said that he "came not to be served, but to serve" (Mk. 10:45).

Another great danger threatening the ascetic is an immoderate desire to dominate. Very rarely does a master find a disciple or a father find a son entirely disposed to give himself to obedience and to renounce his own will to the extent that he, the master and spiritual father would desire. It is true that he is supposed to teach and direct and, if necessary, impose his own will. But these provisos aside, it is nonetheless true that he should not take this as a licence to become a tyrant; he should instead always remain a father, one who begets his son for life and who gives him nourishment. He must respect the freedom of the soul entrusted to him, and the Holy Spirit, the Master within. His fatherly authority is not absolute, because he is only taking the place of Jesus Christ, and the truth is that it is not he who gives life, but God himself who gives it within the soul.

---

8 *Ibid.*, Abba Poemen 127 (70): PG 65, 553D.

He, the human master, exercises an external ministry, as St Paul says, "I planted, Apollos watered, but God gave the growth, so neither he who plants nor he who waters is anything, but only God, who gives the growth" (1 Cor. 3:6).

This is why *apatheia* is necessary if these dangers are to be avoided; further, a life of intense contemplation is necessary to the ascetic-apostle, if he is not to be worried by the many relationships imposed upon him, so Origen is right to insist that such a master of the spiritual life must remain constantly in the temple of God, in other words in ceaseless contemplation. "Wherever the masters are to be found, Jesus is there in their midst, provided that is, that the masters are to be found in the temple and never leave it."[9]

* * *

One quite special form of ascetic life, which escapes all the usual categories and is nowadays rarely to be found in the Church, illustrates more clearly what we have just said about the apostolate proper to the ascetic: the lives of the "fools for Christ's sake".

The thought that Christianity is madness to the wise of this world, and that this world's wisdom is madness in the eyes of God, is one that is dear to St Paul: "If any one among you thinks that he is wise in this age, let him become a fool, that he may become wise. For the wisdom of this world is folly with God" (1 Cor. 3:18-19). We also read that the governor Festus interrupted Paul's discourse, "Paul, you mad; your great learning is turning you mad" (Acts 26:24). St Paul was well aware that his teaching and apostolic life could produce no other impression on unbelievers, and he admitted it candidly, "We are fools for Christ's sake" (1 Cor. 4:10).

This aspect of the Christian life is particularly clear in the lives of the saints who managed to put St Paul's saying, "mad for Christ's sake", into practice in their lives. The Roman Martyrology for 1st July says of St Simeon the Confessor (who died

---

9 Origen, *Hom. in Luc.* 20,1: *Origen: Homilies on Luke, Fragments on Luke*, translated by Joseph T. Lienhard, SJ, FOTC vol. 94 (CUA Press, 1996), p. 84.

about 550, and is a particularly famous example), "He made himself mad for Christ, but by great miracles, God showed the depth of his wisdom."

St Simeon led a very severe ascetic life for twenty-nine years. Only then, under the inspiration of the Holy Spirit, and after having reached a very high degree of perfection, he devoted himself to the apostolic life, so as also to be useful in the salvation of his brothers. Therefore he left the desert into which he had withdrawn and where he had lived until then and returned to the world, but under the appearance of a madman. He came to the help of many, particularly those most rejected and abandoned by this world. In those days, madmen lived at liberty, but in isolation from everyone else, they were joined by all society's rejects. St Simeon gave to each a word which could lead them to Christ. Thus, he still lived outside the world as a true ascetic, even as he also simultaneously exercised a very wide-ranging apostolate. Whenever there was a danger of his being discovered and when his disguise as a madman was no longer sufficient, he would move on, so as to maintain his anonymity. So it was that he led a sort of double life, on the one hand as a madman in the eyes of the world, so that he could live unknown, scorned and humiliated but doing good to all around him, and on the other hand living a completely hidden ascetic life of mortification and prayer, which he practised chiefly at night.

The lives of saints of this kind also help to cast light on other general characteristics of the Christian life. Firstly, they bring out the existence of a double reality in the Christian life, one supernatural and the other natural. The saint lives entirely in the supernatural world, in constant touch with both angels and demons, speaking to them. At the same time he often sees men's thoughts and their secret sins, thanks to the gift of the discernment of spirits. Other men do not live in this supernatural reality, or at any rate do not do so with the same intensity, and they judge the saints according to purely natural criteria. This automatically means that every saint is mad in the world's eyes, a man who has lost his senses. The "fool for Christ" goes further, wearing the mask of madness and so becoming a living example of the folly of the cross, exaggeratedly so, some might say.

CHRISTIAN ASCETICISM

The saint who conceals himself under the appearances of folly preserves himself from the danger of vanity. In St Simeon's "Life", we read that the saint lived in this way "so that his virtue might remain unknown and to avoid receiving men's praises."[10] The often amusing stories of these saints also emphasize how other men's judgements and actions are purely natural and go on to demonstrate where true madness lies. Embracing the life of a madman was a real death for the ascetic, because the mad were the outcasts of society. Despite apostolic contacts, separation from the world was complete, and no form of ascetic life showed more clearly how great was the gulf between the ascetic and the worldly life. Birth, family, country and nature no longer counted for anything. Every Christian ascetic, and not merely the "fools for Christ's sake", will always be looked upon as fools, at least by those who judge them from a purely natural standpoint and put no value on anything but the purely human. It is therefore impossible to justify any modern form of ascetic life which tries to avoid giving this impression — that would be to follow the way of the world and turn away from the folly of the Cross.

"Foolishness for Christ" also shows that the ascetic life does not exclude every possibility of devoting oneself to works of charity, even for one totally separated from the world. The Trappist and the Carthusian, for example, have always to remain separated from the world. He will do it in his own way, differently from the rest of men. It will be unnecessary for him to have much contact with the outside and he will have to practise separation from the world, while practising charity, even at the cost of great sacrifices. If he cannot do this, it is a sign that the time has not yet come for him to devote himself to this apostolate, which is suitable only for one who can give himself completely to contemplation; it shows that he has not yet reached perfection, which can only spread itself abroad as an overflow, *ex abundantia*.

* * *

---

[10] *Life of St Simeon*: *Life of St Salos of Emesa*, by Leontius: PG 93, 1228.

The Ascetic as Apostle

Even when he has become an apostle and spiritual master the ascetic remains under a master, a father, for he must never in his whole life forget that he is a disciple in the spiritual art. The "fool for Christ's sake" who appears even more left to his own devices than the hermit is never completely alone and unchecked. The lives of the saints make it clear to us that each of them always had a companion who knew their secret thoughts, who accompanied them, watched over them and prayed with them during the night.

Every ascetic, unless called by God to a quite exceptional vocation, always remains subject to a master and to supervision, even if he should devote himself to apostolic tasks. And that is why it remains true that even Abbots and masters must, as St Benedict says, never separate themselves from the teaching of Jesus Christ. St Basil put great importance on this constant submission to a master. He said that one should look for someone filled with the virtues, versed in the Scriptures, tranquil in spirit and who loves God. One should entrust oneself completely to such a master for the guidance of one's soul — and St Basil promises that anyone who seriously seeks such a person that they will find one.[11]

But even if it be impossible to find such a person, or if it be impossible to approach him, no acetic may ever dispense himself from submission to a master; if such a one cannot sufficiently nourish his soul, he may, while remaining entirely submitted to him, complement his teaching by reading the Fathers and Holy Scripture. An ascetic who seeks Jesus Christ and his teaching will never fail to find what he seeks. Origen was right to say, "Seek God in the temple of God which the Church is. Seek him among the masters who dwell in the temple and never leave it. If you seek him in this way, you will certainly find him."[12]

---

[11] Basil, *De Renuntiatione saeculi*, 2, 4: *Saint Basil: Ascetical Works, On Renunciation of the World*, trans. Sr. M. Monica Wagner, CSC; FOTC vol. 9 (CUA Press 1950), p. 19: PG 31, 631ff.

[12] Origen, *Hom. in Luc.* 18: *Origen: Homilies on Luke, Fragments on Luke*, as above, p. 77.

EPILOGUE

Mary, Mother of the Church and Ascetics

ALMOST ALL THE MASTERS OF THE ascetic life suggest fervent devotion to Mary, Mother of God, as a particularly effective means to helping us on the way of perfection. This devotion to the Virgin is not just an optional extra offered to us, it has a quite special value in view of the place that Mary, with her extraordinary privileges, has in relation to the goal sought by the ascetic. This fact emerges very clearly from study of the theology of the Fathers.

Mary is the Virgin Mother of the Lord, and this unequalled dignity underlies all her other privileges.

Mary is Virgin, not merely in the sense that she preserved her bodily integrity, but more importantly in the much wider sense that she never incurred the slightest trace of sin.

She is the spotless Virgin. From the fall of our first parents until Mary, there was never a soul so absolutely virgin, since all were marked by sin and were at the very least soiled by the original stain, whereas Mary remained absolutely pure. A special grace also preserved her from original sin; she was conceived immaculate, and that is why, as the Virgin most pure, she was worthy of being the new Eve, alongside Christ, the second Adam.

The virginal purity of Mary is an unequalled model of perfection, put before every ascetic who seeks to ascend to purity and union with God through renunciation and mortification.

Mary is Virgin and Mother. Her virginity is not irreconcilable with her dignity as Mother, rather it was the necessary condition for her womb to bear its divine fruit. Faith in Mary's divine maternity precisely encapsulates the true thought of the Church on the Person of Jesus, since, if she is truly Mother of God, then Christ unites divine nature and human nature in his one Person.

Mary's divine motherhood also in the highest degree implies both the notions of redemption and of perfection: the Virgin bore within her the Word of God and the Son of God, which means that she bore the image of the Father in her womb and in her soul, perfectly reproducing the image of God.

It would have been unworthy of God if his Mother had only borne Christ in her body, without at the same time receiving the Father's Word in her soul. That is why theologians of the first centuries so much insist on Mary's spirit of obedience, her absolute faith and on her self-abandonment which made her worthy of becoming the Mother of God in the physical meaning of the term.

By grace of her virtues, Mary formed the Son of God, image of the Father, within herself in two ways: firstly spiritually, by the perfect abandonment of her soul to the Lord, and then materially, by becoming his Mother; and that is also why she is the one who engendered God, both physically as Mother of Christ and spiritually because she bore Christ in her soul, by virtue of the divine perfections inscribed in it.

Thus it is that Mary became the ascetic's highest ideal. Every exercise of virtue, all that loving questing by a soul in search of God, tends to form Christ in the soul, to make it a Christ-bearer. The Christian soul desires to become, must become, "Mother of Christ", spiritually at any rate. That thought is one that is dear to St Augustine.

The most ancient authors of the Church established a parallel between Mary and Eve, mother of the human race. Eve should have been the mother of life in the true meaning of the world, giving her children supernatural life together with their natural life; but by sin she became the mother of death, and all her children, whose birth was no longer characterized by the life of grace, went through their lives towards the ineluctable death of their bodies. Mary, the new Eve, on the contrary, besides receiving the grace of immaculate virginity also received the grace of divine fecundity and truly became for us the mother of life. After having given us Christ, our life, she, as Mother of the Head, also became Mother of all the members of his mystical body. Mary is therefore both the prototype and the most perfect image of the Church, which brings us all forth into supernatural life.

In Mary, every ascetic, even the hermit who is separated from the world, can see that his efforts to form a new image of God in his soul do not separate him from the Church but, quite the contrary, make him ever more like the Mother of God and the Church which she represents. That is why the ascetic experiences a quite special attraction towards devotion to Mary. It is clear that, far from distancing him from the Church, this honour given to the Mother of God will constantly re-direct him towards the Christian community and the Church, our common Mother.

Mary's final privilege was her assumption to heaven, which the different streams of the Church's tradition variously relate to her divine motherhood or to her immaculate virginity, for that womb which bore the life of the world could not be subject to the law of death; that virginal, stainless body could not fall prey to corruption.

The liturgy itself testifies to the relationship which exists between her immaculate virginity and her assumption into heaven, for the texts of the Mass of the Assumption are taken from the liturgical formulae of the early Mass of Virgins. This fact gains further force if we bear in mind the belief held by theologians of antiquity that the body of St John, Christ's beloved disciple and also a virgin, was also assumed into heaven. St Thomas Aquinas was nonetheless bold enough to reject this theory, which was certainly never universally accepted by the Church, and which no one would nowadays sustain. It does however remain the case that from all we have said, assumption into heaven, body and soul, was especially considered to be an honour given to the virginal life.

The ascetic seeks to free himself from this world's ties; he struggles to purify himself from all sin through an ever more perfect union with God; he seeks finally to realize that mystical ascension of the soul. His model and inaccessible ideal is, once more, Mary, who by her purity, unique in the world, and by her union with God, merited to mount up to heaven, body and soul.

Mary is also the model of the Christian ascetic through her intercession as mediatrix. The Church makes up a communion of saints which embraces heaven and earth; by their prayers and intercession, those who have already attained glory help their brothers still struggling in exile. In the front rank of our intercessors are the martyrs who are Christ's close friends; the choir of virgins, who have won their crown by an un-bloody testimony, joins the choir of martyrs. The Virgin Mother of Christ is at the same time the Queen of martyrs, and on this account is the most powerful intercessor of the Church and Mediatrix of every grace.

The ascetic, too, is called to be an intercessor, and could not choose a more sublime example of this vocation than the Mediatrix of all grace. What his own prayer cannot obtain, he will entrust to the loving solicitude of the Mother of all Christians, whose intercessory power is far beyond that of all the other saints.

Mary received her incomparable privileges by a special gift of God, freely. She did not have to pass through the way of purification in order to reach union with Him, though as a daughter of Adam, even though without fault, she was subject to suffering and death, and had to accompany her divine Son on the way of the Passion. She, then, most perfectly imitated Christ, not only in his Ascension to eternal glory, but also during this life, in the way of the Cross.

Her example, as Mother of Christ and as Mother of sorrows, together with the power of her intercession, makes her one of the great spiritual resources for the disciple and imitator of Jesus Christ. The ascetic who seeks to form Christ in himself and to follow him perseveringly in the way of suffering turns to her with quite special confidence: *Mater Christi, Regina martyrum, ora pro nobis*, Mother of Christ, Queen of martyrs, pray for us.

ABOUT THE TRANSLATOR

GILES CONACHER is a Benedictine monk of Pluscarden Abbey in Scotland (www.pluscardenabbey.org) where of his half-century of monastic life, seven years were spent at Kristo Buase monastery in Ghana, where he was local superior for some years, and where this book was translated. His translations have been published over four decades in four continents.

CPSIA information can be obtained
at www.ICGtesting.com
Printed in the USA
LVHW041950140723
752117LV00003B/526

9 781989 905708